TOP COUNTY CASE CLOSED

By K. N. Messier

Copyright © 2018 K. N. Messier

www.potholepress.com

All rights reserved

Cover design by Nancy

First published on March 28th, 2018

ISBN:
978-0-9992029-3-7

This book is a work of fiction. Names, characters, places, and incidences are the product of the author's imagination. Any resemblance to actual life is entirely coincidental.

No part of this book may be reproduced in any form or by any electronic or mechanical means, including information storage and retrieval systems, without permission in writing from the author.

For more information about formatting, editing, and publishing, please contact:
Austin J. Robinson
+1 (325) 998-0115
arobinson@utexas.edu
www.austinrobinson.ca

DEDICATION

To Simon Moreau, who was a lifelong friend and left this earth far too early. Love ya, buddy.

And to Carrie Baker, who just plain puts up with me! Or I, her. Not sure which! But love you anyway.

TABLE OF CONTENTS

1	THE DRIVE	1
2	OLD BUDDY	8
3	HOME	17
4	POLICE STATION	23
5	DINER	35
6	OLD LOG MILL	41
7	THE SMALLY HOUSE	54
8	NEXT MORNING	63
9	THE CALL	75
10	DOUBLE TROUBLE	91
11	UNEXPECTED VISIT	102
12	RED HANDED	120
13	NEW DAY	132
14	THE SEARCH	145
15	YERKES' HOUSE	159
16	NEW GAME PIECE	174
17	AMBUSH	192
18	SURPRISE	207
19	SHOWDOWN	230
20	NEW BEGINNINGS	244

ACKNOWLEDGMENTS

I would like to thank a special friend who sat at my feet by the woodstove for endless nights as I brought Top County to life. My loving four-legged friend Maple.

I would also like to thank Austin Robinson – owner of Pothole Press – who has burned the midnight oil working tirelessly on editing TOP COUNTY, which by all means was no easy feat. Page by page, he brought this novel to life. Without Austin, you would not be reading this now. I'm proud to call him my friend.

And a huge thanks to Jamie Santamore – owner of Wicked Carnival Productions. I want to thank him for allowing me to work with him and ghostwrite for his project Sins of Man: Rise of Mortis. I wish Jamie the best in all of his upcoming projects.

Finally, I want to thank the great state of Maine. "The way life should be." A wonderful place to live and visit, as well as home to a few famous authors. One of them has the greatest horror genre mind ever – can you guess who?

1
THE DRIVE

Sheriff Patrick Johnson was heading up Route 95 North in Maine during a severe thunderstorm. Although pelted with heavy rain and wind, the sheriff was not thinking about the storm; he was thinking about the last case he was on in the small town of Sandy Creek, Maine. *Sins of Man* he labeled it, and he was glad it was behind him. Now he was focusing on the task at hand: being the new sheriff of Top County.

Top County was a large track of land in Northern Maine. This county was too far north for the Maine State Police to patrol, making it pretty much ungoverned. Due to this circumstance, the county only had a sheriff's department with a dispatcher and room for two deputies whose main job was to patrol the vast amount of land, ranging 6,828 square miles, including the water ways. The magnitude of this jurisdiction made Top County the largest county east of the Rockies. The Top County Sheriff's Department mainly worked the populated areas, while the Department of Environmental Protection worked the outskirts. The DEP called on the sheriff's department to investigate all criminal matters not under the DEP's jurisdiction. This was where Sheriff Johnson was born, so he knew patrolling these parts was no cake walk.

Johnson grew up in Top County and left when he was 18 years old to join the Marines. A bit of a rebel in his teenage years, Johnson remembered getting into a lot of mischief. That's why when he joined the Marines, his father was hopeful they would knock some sense into his thick head. However, his father also knew that meant he was losing help on his potato farm, something that made him unhappy.

That was many years ago. Sheriff Johnson was now in his mid-50s – 53 to be exact. He learned a lot from the Marines. He excelled at everything he engaged in and he climbed in rank swiftly. However, he left the Marines after 10 years, heeding the advice of his mentor, Joe Gordon, who convinced him to join the

Federal Marshals. Now, Johnson was one of the highest ranking federal field marshals, surpassing the rank of Gordon. In fact, Johnson was pushing through this storm in order to see Gordon before continuing north to Top County.

Joe Gordon was the Commander of the Maine State Police, located in Bangor, as well as a federal marshal. Both Johnson and Gordon worked undercover for the Federal Marshals, so when Johnson was given a higher rank than Gordon, it put a small wedge between their friendship. Nevertheless, they remained friends, but decided to take different paths. Johnson went undercover as the new sheriff in small towns filled with corruption, dedicated to breaking up corruption rings to restore order before moving on. Sandy Creek was the last small town he worked in, making it a special place in his mind. There, he uncovered many senseless killings that took place. Luckily, that was all behind him now.

Gordon's role was similar to that of Johnson's. He became an undercover high ranking commander of the Maine State Police in order to uncover any corruption within the state, as well as the political field.

This upcoming meeting between the two was strictly business, as it's been a few years since they've seen or spoken to each other. Sheriff Johnson was wondering how the meeting might go seeing how they would be working together again. *Boy, the rain sure is coming down hard*, Johnson thought to himself as his wipers struggled to keep up with the heavy rain on his truck's windshield. As his faithful companion, Johnson's truck served many purposes: it was his office, his crime lab, his patrol vehicle, and what he drove during recreational activities. For now, it acted as his protection against the storm, gliding along Route 95 at 55 miles per hour due to the low visibility of the road. *WHOOSH*. Suddenly, a souped-up new style black Mustang went flying by Johnson's truck, which made Johnson think he was going backwards.

Johnson was startled, but he managed to get a few letters of the license plate before reaching down to turn on his police lights. He stopped short of turning them on and thought, *Why bother? I'll never catch him safely in this rain.* He decided to let the Mustang go. He wrote the three letters of the plate he happened to catch down on his window pad SMT. About 15 miles later, Johnson saw hazy flashing red lights through the rain, which made him believe that the Mustang that blew by him earlier may have wrecked and required attention. He stopped behind the vehicle and approached it. It was a Subaru Forester with New Hampshire plates – not the Mustang he expected.

A female passenger of the Subaru got out and frantically ran to Johnson's driver-side window. Johnson rolled down his window while she yelled, "SOME CRAZY FOOL RAN US OFF THE ROAD AND CAUSED US TO GET A FLAT TIRE! MY HUSBAND CAN'T GET THE TIRE OFF TO CHANGE IT! CAN YOU PLEASE HELP US?!"

Johnson told the woman to get out of the road and go to the passenger side of his truck. She did as instructed and climbed inside. She was an older woman – about late-60s – and in good shape. He looked at her and said, "Stay put. I'll be right back!"

Johnson grabbed his duster as he got out of his truck and put it on. He made his way to the broken-down vehicle. He approached it with caution, which was usual for federal marshals, and looked through the car windows intently. He saw a man holding his right hand who looked to be in pain. Johnson tapped on the window and said, "You O.K. in there?"

The man rolled his window down and said, "Sorry – I hurt my hand trying to get the lug nuts off my car." Johnson looked at the man's hand, which was bleeding but appeared to just be scraped.

Johnson looked back at the man. "Okay. Come back to my truck. I have more room and an emergency first aid kit. We'll fix you up, get your tire changed, and send you on your way."

"Are you a State Trooper?" the man asked.

"No, sir. I'm a sheriff. And you are…"

"Ken. Ken Lavelle. You met my wife Barbra. We are from New Hampshire."

"Yes, I know. I read your plate. Come on, Mr. Lavelle, sit in my backseat and I'll fix you up."

Mrs. Lavelle was fuming at the thought of the car that flew by, forcing them off the road and blowing a tire. She noticed something in the backseat of the sheriff's large four-door truck. "Sheriff, is that a coffee maker?"

Johnson looked up from tending to Mr. Lavelle's hand. "Why, yes. It is. It's always on – do you want a cup?"

Mrs. Lavelle laughed. "You're kidding, right?"

"Heck no!" Johnson exclaimed before grabbing a paper coffee cup and filling it up for her. "You guys relax and enjoy the coffee. I'll go change your tire. I insist. The rain is coming down hard and you will be safer in here."

Mr. and Mrs. Lavelle agreed to Johnson's

generosity. Johnson hit a switch to turn on four bright spotlights that made the Subaru glow like daylight.

While Johnson was playing with the tire, he couldn't help but wonder about the idiot in the Mustang. After the tire was finished, he put away his tools and got back in his truck. They enjoyed some coffee and staying out of the rain before Johnson asked, "Did you happen to get the license plate number, by any chance?"

"Sorry, we didn't. But we do know it was a loud black car," answered Mrs. Lavelle.

"That's fine. Thank you. Okay! You two can get on your way. Please drive careful."

They both thanked Johnson and prepared for their drive. Johnson cleaned his hands, poured another cup of coffee, and headed back up what seemed to be a deserted highway, thanks to the rain.

2
OLD BUDDY

Sheriff Johnson pulled into the Bangor State Police Headquarters and laughed to himself. *Yep, parking lot full. Have to park half a mile away from the door. Gotta love the rain*, he thought to himself. He entered through the main entrance and walked up to the desk.

"Hey, Sergeant! I'm here to-"

"Is this an emergency, sir?" the sergeant interrupted.

Taken aback, Johnson replied, "No, not at all."

"Then go take a seat and I-"

"It is official business I have with Commander Gordon. He's expecting me," Johnson stated, figuring it was his turn to interrupt.

"Name?"

"Sheriff Patrick Johnson."

The sergeant looked up at Johnson. "Of Sandy Creek?"

"Yes, that's me. Or should I say it was me. I'm the new sheriff of Top County now."

"I heard you resigned from Sandy Creek to take over the sheriff position, considering the last one committed suicide."

"That's enough!" bellowed a stern voice from a distant doorway. There stood a tall man. "Pat! Come on in, old buddy!"

Johnson gave the sergeant a look and walked into a sprawling plush office. He looked around and smirked, "You always did like the finer things in life, Joe."

They shook hands before Gordon let out a hearty laugh and said, "And you never liked to spend money. I see you still have that old truck of yours! I watched you pull in."

"Nothing wrong with her! The old girl does everything I need her to do."

"Ah, Pat, old buddy. You will never change. Have a seat. You need coffee or a little snort of the good stuff?"

"Coffee is fine, Joe. I still have a long way to drive and want to get there by nighttime. By the way, I have a hard time believing Sheriff Taylor committed suicide."

"Pat, my boy, it was a shock to all of us that

knew him. But things change – men change – and he was hitting the bottle pretty hard. Something was bothering him. Who knows what, but it finally caught up with him. It's as simple as that. I would know – I went up there two days ago. The same day it happened. I looked at everything, processed the crime scene where he went off the road, and even checked any open cases he had pending. And nothing! I mean nothing stuck out or looked suspicious! Pat, it's a senseless tragedy, but it's valid and the case is closed! Tell me, my boy, why do you want to go up to Top County anyway? I know you were born there, but God O' Mighty, it's just a few small towns stuck out in the middle of nowhere. The crime is nothing but a few speeders, out-of-town drunks, and some domestics. Nothing will peak your interest for long!"

"Well, Joe, you may be right, but I look forward to a little break. I want to get my parents' old farm and house up-and-running again! Maybe get some hammock time!"

Gordon laughed at that. "Okay, my boy, have fun being bored!"

Johnson finished his coffee before saying, "Joe, I better get going. Do you have the report on Sheriff Taylor's accident?"

"Yes – it's right here. It's a copy, so you

can keep it."

"Thanks, Joe." Johnson put on his duster, shook Gordon's hand, and walked toward the door. He stopped, turned around, and gave Gordon a puzzled look.

"What is it, boy?" Gordon questioned, having seen the look before.

Johnson looked Gordon in the eye and said, "You called it a crime scene."

"What are you talking about?"

"You said you processed the crime scene. The crime scene?"

"Pat, that was just a slip of the tongue, my boy. Just a simple slip of the tongue."

"Yeah, I guess so." Johnson turned toward the door, and then back to Gordon. "Joe, why did you investigate Sheriff Taylor's death? Why not just let his deputy do it?"

"Because he was a good man and I knew he was a friend of yours. I wanted to make sure everything was on the up-and-up because you're my friend, as well. I didn't want a news frenzy. Plus, Deputy Yerkes requested an outside investigation."

Johnson processed Gordon's words for a moment. "Sounds right to me. Good call for the deputy."

"Drive safe, Pat. If you have any questions, I'm just a phone call away."

Johnson gave Gordon a nod and walked out of the office, toward the lobby. He walked over to the sergeant's desk and said, "Have a good shift, Sergeant!"

"Sheriff! Who was this Sheriff Taylor anyways?" asked the sergeant. "He must have been pretty important to get Commander Gordon to fly up to Top County to investigate."

"Just an old friend, is all," replied Johnson.

"Ah, that's why the call went straight to Gordon's office!"

Johnson gave the same puzzled look as before. "So Deputy Yerkes called Gordon directly?"

"I have no idea who called him, but he sure did rush out of here."

"Do you know what time that was?"

"Yes, I do. We keep time records of all incoming and outgoing personal and professional calls. Let's see… it was at 1600. Why? Is that important?"

"No, not at all. I was just wondering how fast the arrival time was," Johnson stated before thanking the sergeant and making a note of his name tag. *Sergeant Mallon.* Johnson headed to his truck.

When Johnson stepped outside, it was no longer raining and the sky was clearing up. He hoped he could make up some lost time and get to Top County before night fall. He looked at his watch and noted it was four in the afternoon. He jumped into his truck and headed north.

Johnson was anxious to get to Top County. He hated unfinished business and wanted to put Sheriff Taylor's case to rest so he could settle into his new life. He couldn't help but wonder what the condition of the old homestead he grew up in was. His parents willed him a massive farm house with over 12 rooms and one large barn with several smaller ones spread out over 1,400 acres of land. There was even a half-mile long driveway. It had been years since he last saw the place.

Johnson's mind quickly drifted back to Sheriff Taylor. He thought about how he was able to get the job for Sheriff Taylor and his wife Mrs. Taylor. It was a dream retirement job for them after the hustle-and-bustle of being a cop and living in New York City for over 20 years. New York was no piece of cake to work in as a detective in the homicide division, so two years earlier when Johnson's childhood buddy Simon gave him the call about going back to Top County to fill the sheriff position, Johnson passed it along to Taylor.

Johnson chuckled to himself at the

memory of Mrs. Taylor yelling in the background of the phone conversation. "HE'LL TAKE IT! HE'LL TAKE IT!"

Damn, they were both so happy to move up north and buy that log cabin on 15 acres of land, Johnson thought to himself. *What the hell happened in two years? What went so terribly wrong that Sheriff Taylor turned to drinking and eventually committed suicide? It doesn't make sense.*

Johnson took an exit off of Route 95, leading him straight into Top County. He took in all of the beautiful yet rugged landscape and noted that not too much had changed. He was on the last stretch of road before entering the first town – a long downward descent with a view of a welcome sign. His mind filled with memories as he pulled up to the Top County Sheriff's Department, which was attached to the town hall. He looked at his watch. 8pm. He wrote it down in his little notepad and did the math. *Let's see: the sergeant said Gordon left at 1600, which is 4pm. That's the same time I left. It's now 8pm. That's four hours of driving.*

Before he could finish his thought, Johnson saw the little diner across the street was still open. He decided to get a bite to eat instead of heading into his office.

Johnson walked over to the diner and couldn't believe that it had the same name as it did when he was a kid. *I'll be darned – it's still Grub & Stuff.* Just as Johnson reached for the diner's door, the open sign turned off. "You've got to be kidding me!" Johnson yelled to the old man inside.

The man turned around and saw Johnson. He unlocked the door and asked, "Can I help you?"

"I see you closed down early, but I was just looking for some dinner to go if you have anything," Johnson answered.

The old man grumbled, "Come on in. I can fix you some soup, chicken, and a buttered roll to go."

"Thank you, sir! I really appreciate it!"

"How many?" snarled the old man.

"Excuse me, sir?"

"Chicken. How many pieces?"

"Oh, four would be nice. And a couple of rolls, too, please!"

While Johnson was waiting, he looked around the diner at all of the old pictures on the walls. He saw one that he remembered. It was of him and his father years ago, delivering potatoes to the diner. Johnson was just a young child. He began to get emotional and reached up to touch the picture.

Suddenly the old man came out from the back. "Here you go, Sheriff."

Johnson spun around to face the old man. "How did you know…"

"Son, I never forget good people. Your dad was the most honest, hardworking man I ever knew. You should be proud."

"I am. You knew my dad?"

The old man burst out in a hearty laugh. "Sheriff, I'm the old man in the picture! Right there!" he said as he pointed to a third figure in the photograph. "That's right – it's me. Hell, I was old then."

Johnson looked at him with amazement. "You're Mr. Hammond? You must be 100 years old by now!"

The old man laughed again before saying, "No, boy. I'm only 92 now. Hush on out of here. I want to close up and go home. We will talk another time." He handed Johnson a heavy bag full of food and said, "It's free tonight. Now scoot."

Johnson nodded his thanks and headed back out to his truck.

3
HOME

Johnson pulled into his long driveway and was partially blinded by the truck headlights shining off the mailbox sporting his last name, minus the "JOH." He laughed to himself, *Guess I'm Patrick Nson now!* He was tired from his long trip, but a flood of memories entered his mind and kept him awake. The big red barn came into focus through the overgrown tree limbs bouncing off his mirrors, making the driveway appear like more of a trail than anything. Then the sprawling farm house came into view. It was a welcome sight even though the rag-tag paint condition was in need of serious repair. Johnson saw a pickup in the yard and a light glowing out of the bulkhead that led to the basement. *What do you know – Mr. Auld must be here!*

Mr. Auld was the oldest of Johnson's closest friends and a neighbor who lived down the road. He was the town's fix-it man and made a good living doing odd jobs for people, among other things. Johnson hired him to get the electricity, water, and heat turned back on before he got there so the place would at least be livable until he could start refurbishing and remodeling it.

Johnson walked down the stairs, leading him to the basement through the outside bulkhead. "Hi, Mr. Auld!"

Mr. Auld jumped back and said in a state of surprise, "Jesus chicken shit, boy! You know how to take a few years off a man!"

"Sorry, Mr. Auld, I didn't mean to startle you."

"Bob. Call me Bob. Patrick, my boy, it's good to see you again! You look well," he said as he sucked down half a smoke before going into a coughing attack. "So," he said while hacking, "you're the," *cough*, "new sheriff in," *cough*, "town now?"

"Yes, sir, I am. How are you making out with the house, Bob?"

"Well, kid, I got most of the plumbing fixed. You have hot and cold running water in the kitchen, but just cold water in the first floor bathroom, and none in the other two yet. I just got the heat on, but this old boiler is in bad shape. It might make the winter. Electricity is all good, but it could use an update. It all works except the old backup generator won't start. I brought you a cord of wood for the fireplace if the boiler goes down or for when you lose electricity, which happens a lot around these parts."

Johnson gave a hearty laugh. "I remember that well!"

Bob laughed with him. "Well, kid, I'll be back tomorrow to finish the plumbing and to give you my bill to date. Would you like any more firewood?"

"Yes, about six more cords, if you got it."

Bob looked happy for the business, "You bet, kid! I'll have it here by the end of the week. But now I'll say goodnight. These old bones aren't used to staying up this late."

Johnson walked Bob to his truck. "Have a good night, Bob. And thank you."

"You bet, kid! Welcome back."

Bob drove off and Johnson went into the house for the first time in 20 years. He looked around and thought, *Yikes! Time has not been good to this old house.* It was getting late, so Johnson sat on the chair at the kitchen table – the same chair he sat on growing up as a child. He cleared off a spot on the table and ate his food from the diner. "Dang, that was some good eating," he thought out loud. He proceeded to his father's old study and was amazed to see everything still there, untouched by time. He picked up a picture of his mother and father as he sat in his father's big lounge chair. He wiped off the dust from the picture and ran his fingers gently over the glass frame.

Suddenly, there was a faint knock on the kitchen door. The knock got louder as Johnson began to stir and wake up from his sleep.

"HEY! HEY KID! YOU IN THERE?" screamed the voice on the other side of the door.

Johnson recognized the voice as that of Bob's. He looked at his watch and mumbled, "Are you kidding me? It's 5am." He got up and let Bob into the kitchen.

"Morning, kid! Were you sleeping?"

"Something like that… Bob, you sure are an early riser."

Bob started to laugh, but went into a coughing attack instead. He handed Johnson a coffee cup and said, "Here, kid. I picked this up at the diner this morning. Figured you might need it."

Johnson gave a look to Bob and said, "Well, you thought right!" He savored a few sips. "*Ah*, now that's better."

Bob handed Johnson a piece of paper with some numbers on it.

"What's this?"

"It's my bill to date. I like to keep things square and even as we go along, kid."

Johnson looked at the paper. "$150? Bob, this can't be right."

"Well, that's the bill! And there's no way I'm lowering it, so don't try your city slicker shit on me, boy!" Bob said robustly.

"Lower?" Johnson said with confusion. "Bob, it's too low for all the work you been doing around here!"

"Nonsense, kid! It gives an old lonely guy a purpose! I'm more than glad to do it." He grabbed the paper out of Johnson's hand and scrabbled a new price down. "There, happy now?"

Johnson read the paper and laughed, "Okay, Bob. You win. $155, it is. Cash or check?"

"Cash, my boy, cash."

Johnson reached into his pockets and pulled out some crumpled up money and counted it. "Bob, here's $135. I'll get you the other $20 later."

"Fine, fine, my boy," Bob said as he grabbed the money. Then he mumbled, "I got work to do. See you later, kid."

Johnson went into the kitchen and looked around. He was happy to see everything was still intact and all the furnishings were still in good shape. He took a quick look around at all of the updates the house needed. He jotted down a few things and plugged the refrigerator in. *Wow,* thought Johnson, *it started! Now to see if it gets cold!* He looked at the time and began to get ready for his meeting with his friend Simon Moreau at the station.

Johnson waved bye to Bob and headed out to the station. He got to the end of his driveway just in time to see a black Mustang go roaring past. "I'll be damned! It's my highway buddy! I'll check on you later – I have business to attend to right now," Johnson mumbled to himself.

He pulled up to the Top County Sheriff's Department. He looked straight at Mayberry – a small building attached to the side of town hall – and chuckled. "It's aged, but it's well kept."

4
POLICE STATION

"Hey, old buddy!" Johnson heard behind him. He spun around to see his old friend, Simon Moreau. Simon looked tall and rugged, showing signs of wear. He was still a very formidable man at 53 years old. Simon worked as the Top County Fire Marshal, meaning he was in tip-top shape. He was also the chairperson of the town committee.

"You old son of a bitch! You haven't changed a bit. Except maybe a little uglier!" Johnson replied.

Simon laughed and fired back, "I see you still wear that want-to-be cowboy hat! And you still drive that beat up old truck! Don't sheriffing pay enough?"

"Ha-ha. Don't let the old girl fool you – she still gets the job done!"

They shook hands and said, "Good to see ya again" at the same time.

"Pat, I see your grip is as strong as ever," Simon said.

"And you're still tall!"

Simon's face got serious. "Wish it was under better terms, my friend."

Johnson's face switched to its typical curious state. "Better terms? Do you mean because of the passing of Sheriff Taylor?"

"Pat, it's more than that. There is some weird shit happening around here lately."

"I figured something was up because you pushed awfully hard to get me to take the sheriff position. Why don't you start at the beginning?"

"Okay, Pat. I do not believe Sheriff Taylor committed suicide. I can't tell you why I feel this way – I just do. For one, why was the fire station and rescue called in after the state police? They were on scene 20 minutes before we even got the call, according to the police dispatch logs. That seems odd, very odd, to me."

"I don't know why, but I will look into it. It could be because a police officer was killed and they wanted to secure the scene. How did you get to look at the police dispatch log?"

"I asked Betty."

"Betty? The police dispatcher?"

"Yes, Pat. She is good people and was very upset over Sheriff Taylor's sudden death."

"Anything else, Simon?"

"Yes. My department has had a rash of unexplained fires in old, abandoned barns and buildings that are way out in the woods. These structures are pretty much forgotten by the locals. The strange thing is that the fires are set to completely destroy any signs of accelerant being used, along with anything that was inside the buildings."

"In other words, it's not kids playing with matches?"

"Exactly."

"Okay, Simon. Does anyone else know about how you feel?"

"No, I kept it to myself until you got here. I figured you would want it that way."

"Okay, let's try and keep it that way for now."

"You got it, Pat. Well, we should head in before the welcoming committee shows up."

Just then, a familiar engine sound came roaring by. A black Mustang came into view. "Hmm, a souped-up Mustang is rare in these parts. Who owns it?"

Simon shrugged. "I have no idea, but I've seen it around a few times. Why?

"No reason – I just think it's odd."

Johnson and Simon walked into the town hall, proceeded down a hallway to the third door on the right, and walked in. There were two desks facing each other and a small jail cell on the side of the door. Johnson thought to himself, *You got to be kidding.*

Simon must have noticed Johnson's eyes because he said, "What do you think, Pat?"

"I have seen bigger broom closets than this station."

Simon chuckled and walked around a corner to unlock another door to a much bigger room. There was a large mahogany desk full of clutter: pictures of Sheriff Taylor and his wife, a thermos, a coffee cup, and scattered files. Also in the room were books on the bookshelf, Sheriff Taylor's spare uniform, and other personal items.

Simon looked at Johnson. "Looks like he's coming right back, doesn't it?"

Johnson nodded.

"Pat, it's untouched just like you asked. Been locked since the day he died."

"I'm glad you called me when you were at the accident scene so we could preserve the only pieces of evidence we might have," Johnson responded

"I knew something wasn't right. Anyways,

I changed the locks like you asked and didn't touch anything. But let me tell you – boy, did it piss off Deputy Yerkes. Betty understood, but Yerkes went wild. At least the council has the final say in things when it comes to the absence of the sheriff."

"Speaking of Deputy Yerkes, where is he?"

"Out on patrol. He knows a replacement sheriff is coming in today and he isn't too happy about that. He thinks the job should have gone to him."

Johnson looked down at Sheriff Taylor's desk and asked, "Any reason why he should not have gotten the job? He is acting sheriff right now, right?"

"Yes, Pat. But he is young and wet behind the ears. Of course he knows everything, but he has only been in law enforcement for three years."

Johnson laughed. "Yeah, I know the type. Did Commander Gordon come down to the station when he showed up to look into Taylor's accident?"

"No. He flew into the accident scene and talked with the state trooper who was already on the scene."

"And what time was that, about?"

"I noted the time in my log book. It was 6:15pm on the dot. Why?"

"Never mind that for now, Simon. Tell me what time the accident took place."

"Taylor radio'd in for help at exactly 4:30pm, according to Betty. Why? What's with needing all these times? What are you thinking?"

"Nothing. Nothing at all. Just trying to get a time frame of how things unfolded. That's all there is to it, Simon. Tell me, why is the station in the town hall? What happened to the side building where it used to be?"

"Roof leaked really bad one night and when the workers came to look at it, they said the walls were full of asbestos. The town didn't want to spend the money to clean it out and redo the station."

Johnson just gave his typical look and mumbled, "Wonderful."

An older, well-kept woman walked into the office and paused for a moment. Her eyes started to tear up.

Johnson looked at her and said to Simon, "I don't believe I've had the pleasure of meeting your friend."

"Please excuse me – I have not been in this office since… since…" she started to say.

Simon jumped in with, "Now, now Betty, it's okay. I know you and Sheriff Taylor were good friends, but I would like you to meet a very good friend of mine. Top County's new sheriff, Patrick Johnson. Pat, meet your-" Simon paused. "-well… everything. Betty does it all around here. From dispatching to processing and everything in between."

Johnson walked over and shook Betty's hand. "Sorry about the loss of your friend. I know you liked him very much and he liked you just as much. Every time I talked with him, he mentioned how wonderful you are, Betty. He was a very good friend to me, as well. I hope you can give me a chance to fill his shoes, and I hope you stay on as the dispatcher because I'm going to need all of the help I can get. I can't think of a better person than you, Betty."

Betty was relieved by the gentleness and calmness of Johnson's voice. With tear-filled eyes, she said, "Oh, yes! I want to stay on! I love this job and Sheriff Taylor always said you were- are, I should say, a good man. I'm sure you will be a great sheriff. He told me when he moves on, you would more than likely be his replacement – he just never told me how ruggedly handsome you are. Boy, I wish I was younger," Betty said with a grin.

Johnson said, "Well, Betty, I do believe you made me blush."

They all laughed. Betty jumped to her work

mode and said, "Okay, fellas, I'm gonna let you talk. I'll go get the coffee on and check on Deputy Yerkes"

"Pat, that was very nice how you calmed Betty. She really is good people and an asset to Top County."

"Thank you. What's Betty's last name?"

"Truman. Betty Ann Truman."

Johnson looked surprised. "Do you mean Frank Truman's daughter?"

"That's correct. As you know, after the Trumans' divorce, Betty moved with Mrs. Truman to Connecticut."

"Yes, I think I remember that. I was just around 10 or 11."

"Well, jump ahead a few years after you left for your stint in the military: Betty moved back after she found her mother dead of a prescription overdose. She figured there was no reason to stay in Connecticut. Plus, Mr. Truman needed the help for his logging operation. *Shhh*, here she comes."

Johnson nodded.

Betty entered the office. "Sheriff, how do you take your coffee?"

"Four creams, Betty. And please call me Pat."

"Okay, Pat, I will. Unless it's police business."

Johnson laughed. "Fair enough, Betty."

"I got to get back to the fire station," said Simon. "Pat, I'll catch up with you later."

Johnson and Betty said bye, and Simon left.

Johnson walked around Sheriff Taylor's old office imagining it as his new office. He felt out of place. The first thing he noticed was that there was no booze anywhere to be found. Nothing was out of sorts, not even in the reports made right up until the day of his death. *Hardly the sign of a drunk whose life was crumbling around him*, Johnson thought to himself.

Then Betty burst through the door with Johnson's coffee and some boxes. "Where do you want to start packing?"

"Just set my coffee and the boxes down on my desk. I need to ask you a question that might upset you. But I have no choice. Did Sheriff Taylor drink?"

Betty looked at Johnson with that don't-fuck-with-my-friend look and quipped, "Yes, a very little at home. To help him sleep. He loved his wife and I'm afraid they may have been having troubles. It was hard for him to sleep, so he had a small amount of whiskey to relax at night." Then with force, she said, "And NEVER, EVER on the job."

Johnson decided not to push the issue any

further. "Thank you, Betty. Please close the door on your way out. I would like to go through the office before we start packing his stuff up."

Betty was quick to say, "I understand. I'll be at my desk if you need me." As Betty was closing the door, she said in a quiet voice, "Thank you, Pat."

"For what, Betty?"

"Believing in him."

Johnson nodded, then heard a loud rumble coming from outside. He looked out of the window to see the black Mustang driving really slow past the town hall, revving the engine. Johnson thought, *Sounds good – a lot more engine than any money around here could buy. My little black Mustang, I will see you soon – you can bet on that.*

Johnson took a seat at his new desk and looked around. "Okay, buddy, talk to me. What did you leave for me as a clue," he said aloud. He reached for his coffee cup and spun it around to reach the handle, understanding that Betty placed it that way on the desk because she was facing the other direction. He then looked at Sheriff Taylor's coffee cup, which was half-full with the handle facing away from him. Johnson got an odd feeling and wondered, *Why would the handle be facing away from him?* He smelled the coffee for any hint of booze. *None. That's a good start.* He decided to bag the cup so he could dust it for prints later.

He noticed a lot of newspaper clippings from the time Taylor busted a king pin drug lord about 10 years ago in New Mexico when he was about to retire from the NYPD detective department. It was the last case he was working on and it brought him all the way down to that state. In fact, it was Taylor's direct testimony that put the drug lord away for life. The last clipping in the pile read, "DRUG LORD TORRINGTON DELL SENTENCED TO LIFE, PUT AWAY BY A RETIRING DETECTIVE FROM NEW YORK CITY, DETECTIVE ANDREW TAYLOR. DELL THREATENED REVENGE AGAINST TAYLOR AS HE WAS LED AWAY FROM THE COURT ROOM IN SHACKLES."

Johnson thought it was odd for the old clippings to be out. He decided it was something he should look into. He picked up the phone to call a friend in the marshal's office, but a little voice in his head told him to hang up. He got up and walked over to the door. He looked through the peep hole and saw a clear shot of both desks. He returned to his desk and muted his cell phone ringer. He called his cell phone with his desk phone, put down the receiver, and walked back to the peep hole to see Betty notice the extension light glowing. She slowly picked up the receiver and put her hand over the mouth piece to listen. "Shit," Johnson said aloud before he hung up his cell phone and watched as Betty looked right at the door.

Great. She's either nosy or corrupt, thought Johnson. On second thought, *No, she's pissed about Taylor's passing and wants answers. Yeah, I'll go with that one for now.* Johnson headed back to his desk and checked out the rest of the room. He found nothing out of the ordinary. He did a microphone sweep for electronic bugs – nothing. Johnson called in Betty to his office. "Betty, let's box this stuff up, label it, and put it in the police holding area."

Betty laughed. "That would be the broom closet."

Johnson also laughed. "Okay, will it all fit?"

"Yes, it will fit. It's a big broom closet."

"Well then let's get it done, Betty. I'm getting hungry!"

It took them about an hour to finish. After they were done, Johnson asked Betty, "You want anything from the diner?"

"No, Pat. I bring my own lunch. You go enjoy yourself," Betty answered.

"Ten-four, Betty."

5
DINER

Johnson walked across the street to Grub & Stuff. When he got through the door, he immediately noticed he was the center of attention. "Small towns," he mumbled. He grabbed a seat at the end table that faces the door and sat down. The waitress walked over to Johnson. She looked to be about 40 years old, 5'5" tall, 135lbs, and had red hair.

"May I help you?" she asked.

Johnson gave her a smile and looked at her name tag. "Yes, you may, Tim."

She gave him a dirty look. "It's Timber! Not Tim."

He gave her a smug look back and pointed at her name tag. "Well I'll be damned! The 'ber' fell off!" he laughed. "I know the feeling."

"Oh, and how's that?!" she quipped back.

"A story for another time. I'm hungry!" Johnson replied. Timber handed him a menu and he handed it right back to her. "I'll have two BLTs with mayo and pepper. No salt. And a coffee, please!"

"Coming right up, cowboy."

Johnson was reading the placemat when Timber came back with his coffee. "So, cowboy, you're the new sheriff in town?"

"Yes, I am. How did you know?"

"Oh, a little birdie told me," she said with a twinkle.

"Tim, do me a favor and tell Mr. Hammond that the chicken was fantastic."

"Glad you liked it! Because I made it!"

"Well, it was mmmm-mmmmm good!"

Timber smiled and said, "Be back in a few with your BLTs. Oh! Would you like a pickle and chips with that?"

Johnson nodded.

Suddenly there was a loud screeching sound from two chairs being pushed back. The culprits were two large men getting up from their table. They walked over to Johnson and one of them said, "So you're the new sheriff in town, huh?"

"Don't look like much of a sheriff, Willy," said the other one.

"Why Wally, I think you're right." They

both laughed.

Johnson looked down at his placemat and wasn't amused, but he hid it well. "May I help you two with something?"

"Yeah, you an old drunk like that old geezer Taylor was?"

Johnson glanced around the diner and could tell the people were uneasy with these two. He knew he had to refrain from going overboard. He got up slowly, put his head between theirs and whispered, "No, I'm a fucking trigger-happy nut job that does not appreciate when two fucktards try to ruin my lunch."

He sat back down and pulled his gun out enough so only the two men could see it.

They backed off and Wally said, "Come on, Willy, let's get out of here."

As they left, Timber brought over Johnson's lunch and asked, "Friends of yours, Sheriff?"

"Nope, not yet," he replied.

"So, cowboy, you find a place to stay yet?"

"Yes, I'm all set! I'm moving back into my old house – the Johnson Farm."

Timber looked puzzled. "That's been empty for years. Are the deceased Johnsons your parents?"

Johnson stood up, threw a $20 bill on the

table, and nodded. Then he said, "Can you box this, please?"

Timber could see he was slightly agitated by her question. "Yes, I'll be right back." She walked to the back and returned with his food all ready to go. "Here you go, cowboy."

While Johnson was walking toward the door, a couple of patrons said, "Welcome home, Sheriff!"

He nodded back to them and then heard Timber shout, "HEY! YOU GOT A FIRST NAME?"

Johnson paused for a second, turned around, and walked out while saying, "YEAH, IT'S PATRICK."

After he left, Mr. Hammond came out from the back of the diner and said, "Timber, I've seen that look before."

"What look might that be, Mel?" asked Timber with a glow.

An elderly couple known as the Tuttles looked up. Mrs. Tuttle smiled and said, "Timber, that's the same look I gave Mr. Tuttle the first time I laid eyes on him. That was 55 years ago."

Timber bunched up and let out an *aaarrgghh* before saying, "I got dishes to do."

Back at the station, Johnson was asking Betty about the whereabouts of Deputy

Yerkes. "I would like to meet and speak with him."

"Sheriff, he's on patrol up north. Would you like me to call him back to the station?"

"No, just relay that I want him in the office at 8am tomorrow. Do you know anything about where my police radio for my truck might be?"

"No, sir, but I will get right on it!"

"Thanks, Betty. I'm heading out. I have a few things to do. Just call my cell phone if you need to reach me. Other than that, I will see you tomorrow."

"Will do, Sheriff. See you later!"

Johnson headed out toward his house while eating his BLTs. He caught himself thinking about Timber. They were good thoughts – the kind that made him wonder if she was single. He laughed to himself and thought, *First day in town and already smitten.* He pulled into his driveway carefully, maneuvering the steering wheel to avoid knocking off his mirrors with the overgrown trees. *Dang, I got to get them cut soon.*

He parked his truck and took a little walk around the once-manicured yard. Now it looked like a wild hayfield that time forgot about. He pried open the door that used to be the one to the garage, where everything got fixed. He remembered how much time he spent in there back in the day. He was amazed that everything was still in place – not a single tool missing!

"Mr. Auld sure is a good neighbor," Johnson said aloud. He closed the door and headed to the house to see it in the daylight and make a battle plan on its rehab.

He found himself drifting back in thought to the diner and that pretty little redhead. *Boy, she sure looked good*, he thought to himself. Then he snapped back to the task at hand: housework. He cleared a spot on the living room table so he could at least have a place to eat. He grabbed a Narragansett beer out of the fridge, cracked it open, and sat at the table before quickly drifting off in thought again.

Suddenly Johnson's cell phone rang. "Hello, Sheriff Johnson!" said the voice on the other end. It sounded like a very excited Betty.

"May I help you?"

"It's Betty! Deputy Yerkes is requesting backup at the old log mill off of Old Log Mill Road. Do you know where that is?"

"Yes, it's off of Timber Wood Road."

"Yes! Ten-four and code one, Sheriff."

"On my way. And Betty – any word on my radio and scanner?"

"Not yet, sir. But I'm on it."

6
OLD LOG MILL

Sheriff Johnson made record time to the old log mill. *Shit*, he thought to himself, *this place was creepy when I was a kid, but now it's downright scary.* He saw Deputy Yerkes' patrol vehicle and pulled up next to it. He did a quick scan of the area, saw nothing alarming, and got out of his truck to check out Yerkes' vehicle. He saw the key still in the ignition. *That's odd. Better call Betty.*

"Hello?"

"Hey, Betty! It's Pat."

"Is everything alright?!" she asked hurriedly.

"Yes, Betty – so good so far. Now shush and listen. Text me Yerkes' cell phone number immediately. But, Betty, do not attempt to contact Yerkes. I'll explain later. Ten-four?"

"Ten-four, Sheriff. Text is on its way."

Johnson received the text and entered Yerkes' contact information into his phone. He made sure his ringer was turned off as he headed into the main entrance of the mill.

The mill had been abandoned for many years, and time was beginning to win along with mother nature. He spotted the administration building and headed for it. When he got to the door, he noticed it had been pushed open recently. He could tell because the old ceiling tiles that fell behind the closed door had been pushed back by the opening of the door.

Johnson knew nothing about Deputy Yerkes, except for what he was told from Simon, which wasn't much. Other than that, he only knew about Yerkes' report on Sheriff Taylor's death. His head was filled with what-ifs and *Why meet out here?*

Johnson yelled, "DEPUTY YERKES! IT'S SHERIFF JOHNSON!" But nothing – no response.

Johnson proceeded further into the building and yelled out for Yerkes three more times. "Okay, plan B," he said to himself. He took out his phone and called Yerkes. He listened for a ringtone. He eventually heard something coming from another part of the mill. He made his way there cautiously until he heard the ringing stop. A voicemail picked up on his end of the line, keeping Johnson on full alert. All of his senses kicked in that something was wrong.

Johnson called Yerkes' cell again and listened. The ringer was louder, so he knew he was closer. The ringing stopped just as he came to a closed door. He looked at it, top to bottom. He saw spider webs, telling him that the door had not been opened in quite some time. *Either there's another way in, or it's a trap*, Johnson thought. *Ah, screw it.* Johnson kicked the door open with full force. The room was well-lit from all the windows on the back wall, but it was empty. Nothing but garbage. Johnson knew the ringing came from inside the room, so he assumed Yerkes was playing games.

He decided to call Yerkes again. It started ringing from inside the room. With a quick search, Johnson found the cell phone on the crud-covered floor. *Did Yerkes drop his phone by mistake?*

Johnson picked up the phone and crawled through a busted window opposed to the way he came. He had a hunch that it was the right way to go. He ended up in a small courtyard that seemed to once be a lunch area. He saw a flashing light across the yard, so he walked toward it with his gun drawn. He saw a man lying on the ground motionless. The area seemed clear, and the body seemed to be that of Yerkes.

The man was bleeding from the back of his head. He was alive. Johnson looked at the wound and chalked it up to Yerkes taking a good hit to the noggin. A quick search of the man's wallet assured Johnson that this was the body of Deputy Yerkes. Johnson attempted to wake him up. Eventually, Yerkes started his journey back from la-la-land.

"Welcome back, Deputy. How many fingers am I holding up?"

Yerkes was still groggy. He whined out, "Four."

"Well, Deputy, that's right. Now come on! Let's get you to your feet so we can get out of here before it gets dark."

They made their way back to the vehicles. Yerkes seemed to be coming around good at this point. Johnson pulled a camping chair and first aid kit out from behind his truck. "Here, Deputy, take a seat while I tend to your wound."

Yerkes complied and Johnson cleaned him up and bandaged the wound. "There! How you feeling?"

"Not too bad. But I feel like I was hit with a 10lb hammer. I could use a coffee."

"Coming right up!" Johnson went into the back of his truck and poured two coffees. He handed one to Yerkes.

"Wow, this is still hot. One hell of a thermos, Sheriff Johnson – I presume."

"You presume right! And no thermos – I have a built-in coffee maker in my truck."

Yerkes peaked in the truck. "I'll be damned! You do!"

They both laughed before Johnson said, "Okay, time to get you to the hospital to have your head looked at."

Yerkes jumped up. "Fuck that! I have had worse snowmobiling!"

"Sit back down and rest for a bit. Tell me what the hell you were doing out here and who slugged you."

"So you're the famous Sheriff Johnson, huh? Heard a lot about you. Pretty good cop from what I understand."

"I do my job. That's about it. Nothing more, nothing less. Now let's get back to why you were out here. Can't be routine patrol this far out."

Yerkes took a sip of coffee. "No – not usually. But we have been having a rash of unexplained fires with abandoned, out-of-the-way mills and barns lately. So I've been poking around this one a little."

"Yes, I heard about the fires from the fire chief. Go on."

"Well, I got here and noticed the door on the main entrance was pushed open. So I went to check it out. I went inside one of the rooms and from there I could see some activity below on the court. I worked my way closer and saw two fairly large men carrying a bag of some sort. So I decided to call Betty and ask if you were active as the sheriff yet. When she told me you were, I asked her to radio you to get you out here in a hurry. I snuck up on the men to get a closer look and find out if I know them. Then I heard a phone ring in the room. That's when I realized I dropped my cell phone. Then *WHAM!* That's all I remember until you showed up. All I can think of is when I turned to look at the room, someone clobbered me on my thick skull."

Johnson began to think, *Okay, so far everything fits.* "Any ideas on what happened after that?"

"No, sir. Other than that, I clearly interrupted something they were doing that they didn't want to get caught doing."

"They could have killed you, but they didn't. Which means they are not killers. Here's your cell phone – I found it when I entered the same room as you. Look through it and see who called you."

Yerkes took his phone and looked through his call list. "I have a few calls from a number with a 564 area code, and one from a restricted phone number. The restricted call was followed by the three local calls."

"The 564 number is mine. Save it into your contact list. You ever get a restricted call before?"

"No. Never."

"Hmm, that's interesting. A restricted call right before someone knocks your noggin. You up to a little walk to see if we can find out what the two men were up to?"

"You bet! But can I get a coffee top-off first?"

"Sure thing, Deputy." After pouring the coffee, Johnson accompanied Yerkes into the mill to see if they could find anything.

After a brief search, Johnson decided that Yerkes should have his head checked. They left the mill and headed to the hospital as a precautionary measure. Everything checked out – no concussion.

"Deputy, go home and get some rest. Take tomorrow off."

"I'll take you up on going home today, but

would rather work tomorrow."

Johnson looked at the doctor, who gave him an *okay* nod. "Tell you what, if you feel up to it then I'll see you at the station around 8am tomorrow. Go home and get some rest tonight and see how you feel in the morning."

It was getting late for Top County. Everything pretty much closes around 8pm. Johnson took a dash over to the diner to see if he could get a few answers. He had a hunch about the incident at the old log mill and figured the diner would be a good place to start.

Just as Johnson grabbed the diner door, it opened. "Excuse me," he said to the elderly couple exiting the diner.

The couple looked surprised and the man said, "Look, ma, it's the Johnson kid all grown up!" She smiled as they walked away.

Johnson almost stepped into the diner when he heard the lady say, "Sonny?"

Johnson turned around to face her. "Yes, ma'am?"

"Be careful up here. It's not the same." She walked away.

Timber approached Johnson and said, "Oh, don't pay her no mind. It's not that bad, even though a few strange things have happened lately. Do you want dinner, cowboy?"

"No, no. Just a coffee, Tim. And to ask you a few questions, if I can."

"Sure thing! Have a seat and I'll be right back with your coffee."

Johnson took the same seat he had last time.

Timber walked over and said, "You sure like to take the farthest booth, don't you?" Before Johnson could answer, she continued, "I know, I know. You can see everyone who walks in and your back is safe." She laughed and sat down with two coffees.

Johnson laughed and asked, "I take it Sheriff Taylor sat here?"

"Yep! And every sheriff before him. But..."

"But what?"

"Well except Deputy Yerkes. He sat anywhere as long as he had a view of the courthouse. Except... oh never mind. I'm just exaggerating."

"Tim, go ahead and tell me. I don't think you're exaggerating."

"Why, I do believe you're trying to flatter me. But okay, I'll tell you my silly little thought. Ever since Sheriff Taylor's accident, Yerkes has been sitting at the counter facing away from the courthouse.

Johnson thought that was odd, but kept it to himself. He joyfully responded, "Maybe he doesn't want to be reminded of Sheriff Taylor, so he looks at the other view."

"Cowboy, I do believe you're flirting with me again" Timber said as she swirled her finger in her coffee, then in her mouth before pulling it out slowly. "You wanted to ask me something?"

Johnson was fixated on her and responded with a weak "What? Questions?"

"You said you wanted to ask me a few questions."

"Oh, yes! Yes, I do. The two guys who were in here earlier today – can you tell me anything about them?"

"Hmmm, where do I start?"

"TRY AT THE BEGINNING!" yelled Mr. Hammond through the wall.

"YES, MR. HAMMOND!" Timber yelled back. "Sorry about that, Sheriff, but he really likes them two boys. He thinks they got screwed over, but here's the story. They are brothers who live at the very end of Thunder Row Road-"

"The old Miller place?" Johnson interrupted.

"Yes. They purchased it about three years ago with some money their dad left them when he died. They were a couple of young college hippie-types with big hearts and an even bigger dream. They were very friendly and well-liked by everyone in town. But trouble soon came their way. An out-of-state asshole named Tony Kicker was buying up a lot of land at the time and wanted the Miller place real bad for some reason. But the boys beat him to it, and that pissed him off. He wanted that 300 acres bad. The 5,000 he owned wasn't enough."

"He owned that many acres?" Johnson asked.

"Owns. He runs a logging operation. Anyhow, he tried to buy the land from the boys, but they were not interested in selling because of their own dream. Kicker tried everything, but the boys would not budge. Then the boys got mysteriously busted with a shit load of crack-cocaine. Long story short, the asshole Kicker bought 280 acres from them to pay their legal fees. He paid pretty much nothing for it. He left the boys with the house, the barn, and a small pond all on 20 acres. But the boys were still in big trouble and needed a good attorney. They were looking at a lot of time locked away. The asshole had connections and promised to keep them out of prison, which he did even though they are now both felons with records. And that's how their dream went up in smoke." Timber took a drink of her coffee before continuing, "So they stay pretty much to themselves and try to survive. They are pissed off at the world, hate cops, and are plum mean. I mean, a nasty mean. Most town folks are afraid of them with good cause. Except Mr. Hammond. They like him and he likes them.

Johnson thought about what Timber said earlier. *A drug set up. But why?* "So, Tim, this Kicker guy is more than likely the top tax payer in town now and pulls a lot of strings. Does he hire a lot of locals?"

"No, he doesn't hire anybody from here. Matter of fact, he doesn't do much logging either. He was well-liked at first and everyone put their trust in him. They all thought he was helping them when in fact he gave them loans that he knew they couldn't afford to pay back. So he charged them a high interest rate and collected that only. He pretty much owns them and their house."

"How much interest, Tim? There are laws about loan sharking."

"I already checked into that. He is legal. Just barely. But legal never-the-less."

"Did he get you?"

"No way, cowboy! No one's getting my tiny little trailer on my one acre!"

"I'm going to look into this Kicker guy. See what I can find."

"Better be careful. He is a lot smarter than some small town folk, Sheriff."

Johnson got up and put on his hat. He looked at Timber and said, "'Til now!" He headed for the diner door, but stopped at the entrance, turned, and said, "Do these boys have names?"

"Wally and Willy Smally."

Johnson gave his look and mumbled, "You've got to be kidding." He walked out the door and got in his truck when Timber came running out.

"Sheriff! Sheriff! I made you a coffee for the road! On the house!"

Johnson rolled down his window and said, "Thank you very much, Tim!"

She gave a warm smile and turned away to head back into the diner.

"Tim?"

"Yes, cowboy?"

"The dream. What was their dream?"

"It was a wonderful dream. A special place for special needs kids to come camp and feel normal with no pressure."

"So, a campground?"

"No, way more than that! Way more."

Johnson nodded and drove away.

7
THE SMALLY HOUSE

Johnson rolled down Thunder Row Road just as the sun started to settle. It was a beautiful sunset, but Johnson had other things on his mind. He pulled up to the Smally house. It looked like a house and yard that used to be well-kept, but has since fallen into a state of neglect.

Johnson was promptly met at the driveway by the two large men that poorly greeted him at the diner. Johnson got out of his truck, looked around, and then put his back to the sunset. "Hiya, fellas! Beautiful evening, isn't it?" he asked.

The larger man walked up to him and asked, "What do you want, pig?" in an angry tone.

Johnson kept eye contact with him and

answered, "To talk is all. I want nothing more."

"Fuck you, pig! Get off our fucking land. NOW!"

"Guys, look. I just want to talk and clarify a few things. I'm not here to start trouble for you."

The smaller man, although still quite large, said, "Get off our land or we will throw you off!"

Johnson replied, "Okay, I see we are going to do this the hard way then."

"Tough talk when you have a badge and a gun strapped to your side."

To their surprise, Johnson took his gun out, unloaded it, and put it on the hood of his truck right next to his sheriff badge. "Now, fellas, about them questions I would like to ask you."

The bigger man went to grab Johnson, but wasn't fast enough. Johnson grabbed his left hand and spun it around, placing him in a painful arm twist. He yelled out in pain while the smaller man yelled, "I'M COMING, WALLY! I'M COMING!"

Johnson let go of Wally as Willy lunged at him. Johnson side-stepped him and hit him hard in the stomach with his knee. He fell to the ground like a rotten tree in a high wind.

Wally, while caressing his arm, screamed,

"WILLY!" before he attacked Johnson from behind. Johnson kicked him in the balls, putting Wally immediately into the fetal position.

Johnson walked back to his truck while the two men were on the ground, one groaning and the other sounding like a vacuum trying to suck mud. He reloaded his gun, put his badge back on, poured himself a cup of coffee, and walked past the men onto their front porch. He sat on a bench, sipping his coffee as he waited for the men to compose themselves back to the standing position.

Wally was the first one up. He helped his brother to his feet and then walked up to the porch. "Okay, Sheriff, I suppose you're going to arrest us now for assaulting a police officer?"

Johnson laughed. "Not a chance!"

"Then what do you want?"

"I want the truth, Wally. Were you two guys out by the old log mill today?"

Wally and Willy looked at each other in surprise. "How did you know?" Wally asked.

"I didn't know. It was a hunch. Now what were you two doing there? And why did you knock my deputy's lights out?"

Wally's tone softened. "Is your deputy alright, Sheriff?"

"Yes, he's fine. Just a moon-size headache

and a little scrape." Johnson's voice got firmer as he said, "Look boys, I'm here to help you, but you need to help me. Now what happened at the mill?"

"Why do you want to help us? And how can we trust you? Why should we trust you?" Willy asked in rapid fire.

Johnson sat in silence and sipped his coffee. He looked at the sunset, then back at the Smally brothers.

Wally finally said, "Okay, fine. We spy on a guy named Kicker and his so-called logging operation. But your deputy spotted them – not us. We were worried that Kicker would have hurt him, if not killed him, so we gave him a little love tap on the head. We laid him down in the tall grass and got the hell out of there."

Johnson's face was hard to read and Wally had no idea if he believed them. Johnson replied, "Okay, Wally. And which one of you two called Deputy Yerkes' cell phone?"

They looked puzzled at Johnson's question. Wally finally said, "Sheriff, neither Willy or I have a cell phone, or any phone for that matter. We have very little money and can't afford that kind of stuff."

"Why do you spy on Kicker and crew?" asked Johnson.

"Because we know that dirtbag is up to no

good, but we can't prove it yet. Not that the cops would listen to us anyways."

"Yes, fellas, I heard about your crack bust," Johnson admitted.

"You heard?!" Willy jumped in. "You heard what? A couple of creeps play nice, fool the town, but are really drug lords? Is that what you heard?"

"Simmer down, son – I'm not the bad guy here," Johnson assured him.

"Well, you really can't blame Willy for getting upset. We came up here to Top County to buy a nice spread, and then came some twit who wanted to buy our land. When we said no, the next thing we knew the state police were knocking on our door with a warrant. They found 100lbs of crack-cocaine in our basement!"

Johnson looked surprised and asked, "Wally, was Sheriff Taylor in on the bust?"

"No, he was not in town yet. It was a few weeks before he took over for Sheriff Badger. Sheriff Badger wasn't in on the bust either, but Deputy Yerkes was. The funny thing is: some big time commander from the state police was in charge. He was barking orders. It sounded like they knew exactly where to look."

"Do you have the name of this commander?"

"No, sir, I don't. I only have the name of the arresting office. His name was Mallon, I think."

Willy spoke up and said, "Yes, it was Mallon. A little beady-eyed punk yes-man."

"Okay, boys, I want to keep this between ourselves. So keep your tough guy act up for now. I will be in touch."

Johnson got in his truck. Willy came up to the driver side and asked, "Do you believe us?"

Johnson looked into his eyes, started his truck, and nodded in affirmation. As he drove away, Willy yelled, "BE CAREFUL OUT THERE!"

It was getting late and dark as Johnson headed home. There were a lot of new questions running around in his head. As he pulled up in his winding driveway, he thought to himself, *Hell of a first day back in Top County.* He silently chuckled as he walked into his house and through the kitchen door. He tried the hot and cold water in the bathroom. To his surprise, it worked. *Time for a hot shower.* He removed his shirt and realized it was pretty cold in the house. He started a fire in the fireplace that his father built forever ago.

The fire crackled as Johnson went back to the bathroom. He jumped in the shower and let the hot water run over his head for more than 10 minutes. He kept his eyes closed. Suddenly, he heard a loud banging. *What the hell now!* He jumped out of the shower and looked around. *FUCK! No towel. You dumbass,* he thought to himself. He ripped down the shower curtain and wrapped it around himself.

He grabbed his gun and headed down the hall to hear someone in the kitchen. He jumped through the doorway and screamed, "FREEZE!"

"Shit, Sheriff! You scared the life out of me!" exclaimed Timber.

"What are you doing here?" Johnson asked in a still-alert state.

Timber answered in a shaken voice. "I just thought I would bring you some dinner. It being your second night back, I figured you might have nothing to eat."

"You thought right. What did you bring?"

Timber looked down and started laughing. "New dress, Sheriff?"

Johnson followed her eyes and realized she was looking at his make-shift towel job, which he didn't realize was see-through until now.

"It's okay, I won't tell anyone in town about your secret desires."

Johnson gave her his look and said, "Give me a minute to get dressed. If you want, you can sit in the living room by the fire."

Timber took him up on that offer. As she was warming her hands, she noticed a door with a mirror on it. It was at the perfect angle to see Johnson in the bathroom. *Don't look, don't look,* she thought. *Ah, screw it! Just one little peak.*

She was silent and motionless as she noticed his muscular body. *Mmmm, not bad, not bad at all there, cowboy.* Then her eyes fixated on his many scars, which seemed to cover every inch of his body. They weren't disfiguring scars, but scars that bear a hard life.

She took her attention away from the mirror and looked around the huge living room as she enjoyed the warmth of the fire. She was in awe of how beautiful the living room must have been at one time. She cleared a spot on the coffee table and started setting out the food she brought.

Johnson entered the room and asked, "Enough for two?"

Timber looked up and answered, "Sure is! But it's only spaghetti and meatballs."

Johnson walked over, grabbed one of the tin plates, and said, "My favorite." He began to eat as much as he could.

Timber was amazed at the amount of food he ate. "Do you have any coffee, Sheriff?" she asked him.

Johnson nodded and started to get out of his chair before Timber said, "Sit, sit! I'll get it. You just relax."

She grabbed the dirty plates and headed to the kitchen. "Pat! Call me Pat, okay?" she heard the sheriff call over.

She turned her head over her shoulder and said, "You bet, cowboy."

It took Timber about five minutes to finish the dishes and return with two cups of coffee. She paused, sighed, and said, "Well, Timber, story of your life: you put him to sleep" to herself. She hunted around for a blanket to put over Johnson. She found one, put it on him, and sat down in the chair next to him. She sipped her coffee and wondered if his parents sat in these same chairs together, enjoying the fire.

8
NEXT MORNING

Johnson woke up because of a loud noise coming from outside. He jumped up, tripped over the blankets that Timber put on him the night before, regained his balance, and rushed to the kitchen to open up the door. He saw Bob Auld dumping a load of firewood.

Bob yelled, "MORNING, KID! HOPE I DIDN'T WAKE YOU!" from the cab of his truck.

Johnson looked at his phone and said, "MR. AULD, IT'S 5AM!"

"YEAH, YEAH, KID. I KNOW – I'M A BIT LATE!" responded Bob with a hearty laugh. Then more quietly, he said, "I see you have company! Don't waste much time, do ya?"

Johnson looked surprised. "What do you

mean company?" he said before hearing a voice from behind him.

"Hey, cowboy! It's me. I fell asleep watching you sleep," Timber said as she squeezed by Johnson in the door frame. "See ya later! I got to get my ass to work or I'm going to be late!"

Johnson and Bob watched as she walked away and got into her car. "What an ass she has! Hmmm. Second night in town, kid? Not bad, not bad at all!"

Johnson gave Bob a look and closed the kitchen door. He got ready to head to the station, went out to his truck, and headed down his driveway. He was on the road just in time to catch the black Mustang passing by very slowly. Johnson decided to pull behind the Mustang and follow it. The driver was doing the speed limit, but Johnson wrote the plate number down just in case. Then he headed to the station.

"Good morning, Betty! Mmm, the coffee smells good," Johnson said to Betty as he walked into his office.

Betty responded, "Good morning, Sheriff! I hope you slept okay. Here's your messages. Your radio will be here today. Deputy Yerkes will be in shortly. He stopped a car for speeding on his way in. And your coffee is on your desk already! I seen you pull up to the station and got it ready for you."

"Betty, you're wonderful – do you know that?"

"Why, thank you! And yes, yes I do know that," said Betty, grinning ear-to-ear.

"Can I see you in my office for a few minutes. I need to pick your brain a little." Johnson walked into his office with Betty right behind him. "Grab a seat. Do you remember when the Smallys got into trouble a few years back?"

"Oh my, yes! We could not believe what they did. It shocked the whole town. Though, something never felt right about that case."

"I agree. Is there a file on it around here?"

"No, sir. The state police said it was an ongoing state investigation and took jurisdiction over it. They told Sheriff Badger to stay out of it."

"What ever happened to Sheriff Badger?"

"Oh, he retired and move down to Florida!"

"Thank you, Betty. That's what I heard – I just wanted to confirm it. So Badger was okay with the state police coming in and taking over?"

"Oh, Pat, by that time Sheriff Badger was just going through the motions until he retired.

He really didn't care and was just counting down the days left."

"Did you know the Smallys on a personal level?"

"Oh, yes! They are bright kids and were always pleasant and smiling. They would come down to the town hall and volunteer! They liked to help people. But I guess it was all a cover for who they really are – big, bad, nasty drug dealers! Which is still hard to believe. But how they treat the folks in town now is scary – they're scary! I guess we just never knew them."

Johnson thought to himself, *Or maybe the town let them down when they needed it the most.*

Betty looked at Johnson concerned and said, "Why the interest in the Smally boys?"

"Nothing really. Just had a small run-in with them at the diner, is all."

"You better watch them two. They turned meaner than four junkyard dogs combined!"

Johnson let out a hearty laugh and said, "Okay, Betty, will do! Thank you for the info. Please close my office door on your way out."

Johnson sat at his desk and made a call to his most trusted friend at the Virginia Marshals headquarters – Mike Baker.

"Mike, it's Pat. I need you to do me a favor on the QT."

"Sure, old buddy! What you working on?" asked Mike.

"I need you to run a plate for me. Run a background check on the owner."

"Sure! No problem. But why not just go through your own dispatch? Wait, forget that – I don't even want to know. Just give me the plate numbers."

Johnson laughed and said, "Okay, Mike. It's SMTTTK."

"Come again, Pat?"

"It's Sam, Mike, Tough, Tim, Tool, Ken. SMTTTK."

"That's what I thought you said. Kinda a weird plate. Any idea what it means?"

"No clue. No clue at all. Oh, and it's a New York plate."

"Okay. And when do you need it by? I know, I know – yesterday, right?"

Johnson grinned and said, "Just send it to my personal email, okay?"

"You bet. I'll get right on it."

"Thanks, Mike. I owe you a beer. Talk to you later!"

"Make it a case, Pat! Bye."

KNOCK, KNOCK, KNOCK came from Johnson's door.

"COME IN!" Johnson bellowed.

"Morning, Sheriff!" Deputy Yerkes said as

he walked into the office.

"Hey, Deputy! How you feeling today? I hear you had a busy morning already."

"I'm fine. It was just a little scratch. Had worse falling off my sled. And the traffic stop was just a couple of kids speeding on their way to school. So I just scared them a little and issued a warning."

Johnson looked up at Yerkes and asked, "Scared them, Ben? How is that?"

"Nothing really. It's a tactic I use. I tell them about a few teenage accidents that I've seen. I get a little graphic to shake them up a bit."

"Do you think that helps?"

Yerkes laughed and said, "Probably not, but you got to try something with these kids."

"Agreed. Ben, I want you to give Betty your itinerary for the day and every day until we can get some info on who clobbered you. I'm not trying to babysit you – just want to know where you are at all times. Somebody out there has no problems hitting a police office. There's no telling what they may do next time."

"No problem with that, Sheriff. Sheriff Taylor was a babysitter – up my ass constantly, wanted me to check in every half hour, and so on. Used to piss me the fuck off!"

Johnson noticed the aggression coming

from Yerkes' face and words. "Well, Sheriff Taylor had his reasons, I'm sure."

"Maybe, but I did not like it one bit."

"Duly noted. Be careful out there today. My radio will be in today and as soon as it's installed, I'll give you a shout."

"Ten-four." Ben walked out of the office and gave Betty his planned route for the day before heading out on patrol.

Johnson locked his office door and got Sheriff Taylor's coffee cup to dust for prints. He got two readable prints off of the cup and ran them through the station's database. They came back matched to Sheriff Taylor and Betty. *Nothing out of the ordinary*, thought Johnson, *but the position of the cup still bothers me. Why would it be faced away from Taylor when he was sitting at his desk?* Little details like this bothered him. He was almost like a Columbo minus the coat.

Johnson was deep in thought when Betty chimed in through the intercom. "Sheriff, your radio was just delivered. Sheriff, you there?"

Johnson cleared his head and said, "Yes, Betty. Thank you. I'll be right out."

"Ten-four."

Johnson looked over the radio and told Betty, "Hold the fort down. I'm going to see my old friend at Old Skool Garage and install my radio. If you need me, you know where I'll be. I will call you on the radio when it's done to make sure it's working properly."

Betty waved him off as he headed out to the garage, which was out in the middle of the woods.

Johnson made his way down the long dirt road until he saw the Old Skool Garage sign. He stopped and thought, *Wow, hard to believe I remember that sign when it was new. Now it's all but faded.*

Johnson was greeted by a large dog as he arrived in the driveway. The dog was friendly and looked happy just to see someone. Johnson spent a lot of time at this garage growing up – the owner was sort of a mentor to him. It's where he learned how to fix things and pondered about life.

Johnson got out of his truck and saw his friend torching some metal. He creeped up on him and said, "Excuse me, sir, I'm looking for Sneaker. Are you him?"

The old man didn't stop what he was doing or look up at Johnson. Just quipped back, "Depends who's looking."

"The sheriff, that's who!" Johnson said with authority.

Sneaker didn't budge or look up. Just said, "Are you the new sheriff in town?"

"That's right, I am! And I need to talk to you!"

Sneaker stopped what he was doing, lifted up his welding helmet, and picked his half-smoked cigar off of the car fender. He still had his head turned away from Johnson while he said, "Kid, I would know the sound of that engine from anywhere. How the hell you been?"

Johnson laughed to himself. *There's that word 'kid' again!* "I've been very good. It's great to see you again, Sneaker. How the hell have you been? Still busy as ever, I see!"

"Yeah, kid, real busy. But I'm fine – just getting older. It's great to see you all up and personal instead of just a voice on the phone! And the new sheriff in town, no less. I take it you're going to stick around. So, is this a personal call or business?"

"Both! Two birds with one stone – you always told me."

"That I did, kid! That I did."

"I need to install a police radio in my truck and would like to adjust my fuel rail pressure up on the old girl."

"Why? You going drag racing?"

"No, nothing like that. I just have a gut feeling that I'm going to need it. But first, you got coffee? I need to speak with you."

"Kid, it's your second home – help yourself. What's on your mind?"

"Do you have any idea what the hell is going on around here? Just don't feel right to me."

Sneaker puffed his cigar and said, "Then go with your gut feeling, kid. Has it ever let you down? Come on – let's talk while we work on your truck."

"What do you know about this Kicker character?"

Sneaker looked up at Johnson and said, "He's an asshole. Thinks his farts smell like roses. One of them no-good, sum-bitches that everyone trusts. You be careful of him. He's as two-faced as a prosecutor. Comes up here and starts buying up everyone's excess land."

"Why are the folks selling?"

Sneaker relit his cigar, took a puff, and said, "Kid, they are not selling. They are losing their land to this jackass. He gives out loans to the people he knows can't pay them back. As soon as a payment is late, he calls the note in early and *poof*, another farm or wood lot gone. The prick only does it with places that have a lot of acreage. Or should I say, did. He's got all the land he needs now – and then some! The prick just about gated every dirt road in Top County off so no one has access to the land either."

"The land that Kicker steals – do you know if some of it has old mills or barns or any kind of buildings at all?"

Sneaker rolled his cigar around and scratched his bald head. "Why yes, they do. Come to think of it, just about every parcel he stole has some sort of building or structure on it. Why you ask?"

"Not sure yet. Just one of them gut feelings is all."

"Well, kid, it can't be insurance. None of them buildings are worth a darn. Maybe just for recycled timber. Sure wouldn't be worth the risk of burning them up."

Johnson nodded in agreement.

"I have the radio installed, now. I'll check her out for you." Sneaker called in to Betty through the police radio. "Betty. Come in, Betty."

Betty responded, "How's it going, honey bunch?"

"Good! Betty, baby, how's the radio sound?" Sneaker slyly asked.

"Oh, you old coot! It sounds wonderful!"

Sneaker snickered and responded, "We on for supper tonight at my place?"

Johnson grabbed the mic, "Give me that! Geez, Sneaker, it's a police radio – not a dating machine! Betty, Sheriff Johnson here. Radio works, I take it?"

A nervous Betty said back, "Yes, sir! Ten-four, Sheriff! All clear!"

"God dang, kid, I was just having a little fun with Betty," chimed in Sneaker.

"Yeah, on a police radio. People have scanners, you know!"

"I installed a one-off crystal in the dispatch radio, as well as mine. No one else has it – just us. It's tact four."

"Tact four, Sneaker? How do you know to go on tact four?

Sneaker gave a wise-ass look and said, "Well, Mr. Sheriff, our radios pick it up automatically and alert the user. That would be us. It emits a distant beep when someone on tact four keys the mic, so to not alert anyone listening. But you must switch to tact four to communicate."

"That's why they call you Sneaker. Okay, cool, it just may come in handy someday."

"Kid, that's what Sheriff Taylor said, too!"

Johnson gave his look, closed the hood of his truck, and said, "Truck's done. I have to roll. Talk to you later, lover boy!"

Sneaker chuckled, "Ten-four."

9
THE CALL

Johnson was on his way to the diner when he heard his radio crackle with a very frantic Betty on the other end.

"Sheriff, Sheriff. Come in, Sheriff. It's Betty. Come in, please."

Johnson responded, "Go ahead, Betty."

"Sheriff, there are a couple of hikers from New Hampshire here. They found a decease female body in the woods."

"Keep them there. Call Deputy Yerkes and have him return to the station. I'm on my way. Ten-four?"

"Ten-four."

Johnson mumbled, "No better time to check out the fuel rail adjustment." Johnson slammed on the gas pedal and the old dually came to life and barked over the rear tires. His truck hit 90 miles an hour in mere seconds. He was barreling down highway one – a rural route, but made for speed – with his siren blasting. Then out of the corner of his eye, he saw the black Mustang sitting down a little dirt road. Johnson wondered who would bring a car like that down a dirt road, and why.

Johnson and Yerkes pulled into the station at the same time. They ran into the building while Betty met them at the door.

"Sheriff, Deputy. These are the Lavelles – Mr. and Mrs. Lavelle." Then she looked at the couple and said, "This is Sheriff Johnson and Deputy Yerkes. They will take it from here."

"We have met your sheriff before," said Mr. Lavelle.

Johnson could tell they were both pretty rattled and scared. "Sorry we meet again under adverse conditions, Mr. and Mrs. Lavelle. Would you folks like something to drink?" offered Johnson.

Mrs. Lavelle had a look on her face that Johnson had seen many times before. He knew it was not going to be good. She mumbled, "Tea. Do you have any tea? We would both like tea."

Betty got right to making the tea while Johnson said, "Please, folks, take a seat, breathe, and relax. Tell the deputy and I what you came across and where."

Mrs. Lavelle got hysterical. "RELAX? RELAX? We just saw a naked young girl hanging by her arms from a tree, beaten to death. And you want us to relax?!"

Deputy Yerkes chimed in, "Look, lady, we don't need the drama from you. What we need is the facts!"

Johnson gave a pissed look to Yerkes and said, "That's enough, Deputy. Mr. Lavelle, think you could bring us to the crime scene?"

Mr. Lavelle complied and looked at his wife. "You stay here."

Johnson gathered up the deputy and Mr. Lavelle and they headed to the crime scene. It was 40 miles away from the station, with the last five miles being heavily wooded and slow-going.

"This is as far as you will be able to drive. We have to walk the rest, but it's not that far. Just about 50 yards down that path up ahead," said Mr. Lavelle.

"Okay, you stay here with the truck and wait. My deputy and I will go investigate," replied Johnson.

"Glad to. This type of shit isn't for me!"

Johnson nodded and headed down the path with Yerkes. After a short walk, they came to a small clearing. They saw the victim hanging by her wrists via rope tied to a tree limb. Her feet were about a good foot off the ground. Her body was battered, beaten, and mutilated to a bloody pulp.

Yerkes was stunned, as if it was his first time at a horrific scene such as this one. "What the fuck, Sheriff?!" Yerkes let out before he ran into the woods and started puking.

Johnson had seen some pretty bad murder scenes in his time, but this one was right up there at the top as being the most brutal. He started to investigate the body while Yerkes regained his composure and stared at the body. "What do you see, Deputy?"

"I see a young girl, maybe 18-20, badly beaten by some sick fuck, sir. That's what the fuck I see!" quipped Yerkes.

"She was whipped to death. See that cut tree stump over there? And the way the clearing is made? This was a planned attack that she more-than-likely walked into not knowing it was going to be the end of her life."

Yerkes just looked at Johnson and said, "Walked into? Sheriff, what the fuck does that mean?! Are you nuts? Who would walk into something like this!"

"I don't know all the answers, yet. But look at her clothes."

"Yeah, so what?"

"They are folded neatly. Even her underwear and socks."

"Are you saying this was a date gone wrong?"

"Kinda. More like a play session gone wrong. You ever hear of BD/SM?"

"Holy shit! Here in Top County?"

"Go to your cruiser and get some baggies. And the camera. Call Betty and ask her to get the coroner out here, stat. I'll start processing the scene so we can cut the victim down ASAP."

"Ten-four, Sheriff."

Johnson studied the body carefully. She was Black, about 5'6", approximately 125lbs, had long black hair, sported nipple piercings, and had perfect teeth. She was well groomed except for the fact that she had whip marks from head-to-toe, front-to-back. By the looks of how far the rope was embedded into her wrists, she was alive and fighting hard to get away from the brutal whipping.

Johnson noticed something on the ground: a broken electrical probe, of the clamp variety. He looked more carefully at the body. *Dang*, he thought to himself, *I almost missed these burn marks. They are all over her nipples and vagina. This poor girl was not only whipped, but tortured with an electric shock device or stimulator. And by the color of her hands, she was hanging from her wrists for a long time before she succumbed to the brutality of her attacker.*

Yerkes returned with the camera and baggies. He asked Johnson what he wanted photographed. Johnson explained the burn marks and told Yerkes to take a photo of every inch of her body and a few shots of the clearing.

"Okay, Sheriff. Do you have any idea who did this?"

"Very little to go on. Do we have any Black families living in Top County that you know of?"

"Yes, sir, we do. But I have never seen this girl before."

"If I was a betting man, I would say she was from New York." Johnson panned the area and noticed a small and narrow freshly cut path hidden just enough by some tree branches. He walked over to check it out. "Yerkes, bring your camera over here and let me see it."

Johnson placed the camera on a fresh-cut tree stump, which was about three feet high. He looked through the camera to see a perfect view of the body. "Yerkes, whoever did this filmed the whole thing. Here, take a look."

Yerkes looked through the lens and

excitedly said, "Jesus Christ! I'm going to call in the state police!"

Johnson firmly replied, "Look, boy, are you a law enforcement officer or a parking maid? We will handle our own. Understood?"

Yerkes seemed annoyed. He replied, "This is forensic science shit. I know nothing about it! The right thing to do is call the state police!"

"No, Deputy, we will not. I happen to have studied forensic science, and with help from you and the coroner, we will solve this. Are you on board?"

"Fine, Sheriff, we will do it your way. What do you want me to do next?"

"Scan the area – about a hundred yards or so in each direction. Look for anything – and I mean anything – out of place. Including trash."

"Ten-four," Yerkes said before he began sweeping the area.

An old-timer came walking down the path right into the crime scene. He seemed about early 70s, thin and pale, but very spry and moved about like a 50 year old. He walked up to Johnson and said, "You must be the new sheriff! One hell of a way to welcome you to town. I'm Quincy – the county coroner." Quincy held out his hand to Johnson.

Johnson reached out and shook the coroner's hand before saying, "Quincy? That's a good one."

The coroner laughed and said, "It's true, Sheriff. Just like the TV show except I'm Quincy Smith. Here's my card!"

Johnson looked at the card and said, "Well I'll be darned! I'm Sheriff Patrick Johnson and we are not sure who the victim is."

"What do we have so far?"

"Take a look, doc. You tell me," replied Johnson.

Quincy walked over to the body and looked in disbelief, but stuck to the task at hand. He started by slowly examining the victim's feet, looking from top to bottom. He started speaking into a recorder, "Victim was wearing shoes or socks pretty high up and the bottom of her feet are clean with no dirt of any kind. Her soles are soft. City girl, I suspect. Tattoo around her left ankle appears to be barbed wire. No bruising on her inner thighs, so rape may be out of the picture. There is a burn mark — no, make that two burn marks around the vagina caused by some sort of electrical device. Her rib cage shows bruising with the possibility of a few broken ribs, showing she might have been punched while hanging by her arms. More electrical burns around the nipple area of the breasts, and nipples seem to be protruding out more than normal — may be caused by a suction-type device. Her mouth is in a wide-open position — note as odd. Her hands are dark purple from the lack of circulation, no doubt caused by the rope around each wrist supporting her body weight. There are multiple welts throughout the body, appearing to be whip marks with concentrated abuse at the buttocks, back, stomach, breasts, and vagina areas."

He turned back to Johnson. "Sheriff, this is all speculation until I get her on the table, so let's cut her down and get on with it."

Johnson was slightly dumbfounded by this country bumpkin's thorough description.

"What's wrong? Didn't think us backwoods crazies had any smarts?"

Johnson gave his look and simply said, "Catch!" as he cut the rope holding up the body.

Yerkes returned and told Johnson what he had found: a fresh set of tire tracks about 500 feet down a newly cut path leading to an old dirt road.

"Good work, Yerkes. Can you take a few good pictures of them?"

"Already did. And of the path."

"Okay, excellent. Let's help the doc get this body loaded up and I'll bring Mr. Lavelle back to the station. Just one question — can you make a tire cast?"

"Sure I can! Haven't made one since the academy, but I'm on it!"

"Excellent." Johnson then turned to the coroner. "Quincy, if you find out anything new, I want to know about it at any time. I want this poor girl identified quickly."

"I'll pull for her dental records as soon as I get back," replied Quincy.

"Then let's roll! We got a crime to solve!"

Johnson returned to his truck with Mr. Lavelle still sitting inside. "Mr. Lavelle, thanks for waiting."

"No problem, Sheriff. So... what happened to her? Outside of the obvious."

"We don't know yet. Tell me, what were you and your wife doing hiking out this way?"

"You don't think we had anything to do with this, do you? We are both respected Southern New Hampshire University professors. I resent the fucking fact that you think we had-"

"STOP!" Johnson interrupted with authority. "I said no such thing! A girl – a very young girl – was just brutally murdered and you're worried about me asking you a few questions? Now tell me, if that was your daughter hanging there, wouldn't you want a complete and thorough investigation? With no stone left unturned?"

"You're right. Of course. I'm just freaked out and maybe a bit scared. My wife and I research old mills and homesteads – places that time forgot. We photograph them as a hobby, and then try and tell their stories."

"Sounds like a fun hobby, Mr. Lavelle. But why Top County?"

"Top County is one of the few places left that is relatively close to us, and not yet destroyed by kids and progress. This is our second year coming here and we've barely scratched the surface! It's a gold mine for us. Plus, we love it out here. Well, we did – not so sure now."

"Don't worry – we will catch whoever did this."

"It's not just this, even though this was the icing on the cake. But we are finding that some of the old structures have been burnt to the ground for no apparent reason. That's scary in itself!"

"Mr. Lavelle, do you have photos of them before they were burnt down?"

"You bet we do. Tons of them. Would you like to see them?"

"Yes, I would. Do you have them here with you?"

"Yes, they are on my wife's computer. I

can download them onto a memory stick for you when we get back to the station, if you want."

"That would be great. You never know what we might find. You just never know." Johnson grabbed his police radio mic and said, "Dispatch, this is Sheriff Johnson. You read?"

"Loud and clear, Sheriff."

"Betty, go to tact four."

"Ten-four." And then, "Betty here, tact four."

"Betty, I want this investigation kept on the quiet from everyone for now. Especially the local paper. I'm on my way back with Mr. Lavelle. Please instruct Mrs. Lavelle on the hush-hush. The last thing we need is a bunch of publicity to interfere with our investigation. Johnson out."

"Ten-four. Dispatch out," Betty ended.

Johnson turned to Mr. Lavelle. "I hope you understand that I need your cooperation to help keep this under wraps for now."

"I understand. I will help in any way I can."

"Thank you, Mr. Lavelle. On yours and your wife's hiking trips, have you noticed anything odd or out of place or just not right? Anything at all while exploring some of the old barns and mills?"

"Like what?"

"Anything at all. And I mean anything."

Mr. Lavelle scratched his chin and said, "Hmm, not really. Well one thing, I guess. But nothing I would call really odd."

"Let me be the judge of that," Johnson replied.

"Well, my wife and I saw a black car. You know, one of them souped-up kinds. It was on a bumpy dirt road. I thought it was an awful nice car to be out here."

"Was it a Mustang? And have you seen it before?"

"Could've been. But I'm not really up on today's cars. It had a weird license plate. It said SMTT or something like that. But no, I don't think we had ever seen it before. Do you think it's important?"

"Maybe. Did you see who was driving it? Was it a male or female?"

"No, sorry. Just the car."

"Okay, fair enough."

They arrived at the station and Johnson announced, "Mr. Lavelle, here we are. Please have your wife download the pictures for me. Betty will take all your info down so you can go on your way. But if you or your wife remember anything – anything at all – please don't hesitate to call me. Here's my card. Call me directly."

"You bet, Sheriff. You not coming in?"

"No. I have to check on something. Be safe on your ride home."

"Thank you. It was a pleasure meeting you again. Just wish it was under different circumstances. Good luck, and please be safe. It looks like you got a real creep on your hands." Mr. Lavelle exited Johnson's truck and entered the station.

Mrs. Lavelle greeted her husband with worry. He instructed her to download the pictures onto a memory stick. When she asked why, he told her everything. Betty took down their information and copied their driver licenses.

"Mr. Lavelle, here is a copy of the report your wife filled out," said Betty. "Please read it in the case you would like to add something. Then if I could get you to sign it, that would be great."

Mr. Lavelle went over the report carefully and said it looked accurate. He signed it and him and his wife went on their way.

Yerkes entered the station looking a little on the excited side. "OMG, Betty. It was horrific!" He went on to explain the crime scene. Betty looked shocked that something like that could happen in their own backyard.

"Where's the sheriff?" Yerkes asked Betty.

"No clue. Want me to call him?" Betty responded.

"No, that's fine. He wanted me to make tire casts of the marks I found. They're in my patrol car. I'll go get them and bring them into his office." He left and returned with the casts. "Betty, do you find it funny that all this is taking place pretty much when Johnson arrived? I mean, what do we really know about him?"

Betty stared at Yerkes and said, "Johnson is a highly-decorated police officer who has solved some amazing crimes. So you're barking up the wrong tree, Ben. And you're a fool to even think that."

"Betty, calm down. I was just wondering, is all. Besides, Johnson himself told me to look at everything because most times the answer is staring right back at you."

"Ben, that may be true, but I just think you're barking up the wrong tree."

"Maybe. But who else in town is capable doing something like this? The two idiots known as the Smallys?"

Betty gasped, "Oh my god – you don't think…?"

"Well, they are pretty creepy," Yerkes responded.

"You better not do anything without

checking with the sheriff."

"Of course not. Well, I'm off duty now. I'm going to head home. Tell Johnson that if he needs me, I'll come back in."

"Will do. Have a good night. Oh, and Ben?"

"Yes, Betty?"

"You're right. It is a little weird. But I'm sure it's just a coincidence."

"I'm sure it is," Yerkes said with a grin.

10
DOUBLE TROUBLE

Deputy Yerkes was looking to make an impression on the county considering he wanted the sheriff position. So he decided to drive out to the Smally house.

He parked down the road and snuck up on the house. He peeked in the front window to see Willy cleaning what appeared to be blood off of a rope. Then he heard Wally ask, "Willy, you think she's still alive?"

Yerkes squatted down and started to tremble. He thought, *What do I do? What do I do? Call the sheriff?* But then he began thinking about the hero he would become if he was the one to discover the young girl's killers. He began to grin at the thought of all the glory. It was more than he could handle.

He took a deep breath and drew his service

revolver. He kicked in the front door and yelled, "SHERIFF'S DEPARTMENT. ON THE FLOOR NOW. NOW! ON THE FUCKING FLOOR!"

Wally and Willy were caught off guard by the intrusion. Knowing he was outnumbered, Yerkes fired a shot at the floor and continued his yelling. "I SAID ON THE FLOOR NOW! OR THE NEXT SHOT IS IN YOU!"

Both men got on the floor screaming, "WHAT DID WE DO? WHAT DID WE DO?"

"SHUT THE FUCK UP OR I'LL KILL YOU BOTH RIGHT NOW, YOU SICK BASTARDS!" Yerkes kneeled on Wally's back and handcuffed his hands together. Then he pulled a lamp cord off the nearby lamp and tied Willy's hands together. He put his gun to Willy's head and said, "I should put a bullet in your head right now, you sick bastard."

Willy started, "Deputy, what did we-"

WHAM. Everything went black. Willy was out cold. Wally screamed, "YOU SON OF A BITCH – I'M GOING TO KILL YOU!"

Yerkes laughed, pointed his gun at Wally, and said, "Big man, you want your head smashed in with the butt of my revolver, as well?"

Wally was silent.

"Ah, the big silent type. Good! Stay that way until I give you permission to speak!" Yerkes said with a twisted look on his face. He thought to himself, *I do believe I am enjoying this.*

Then he looked down at Willy to see blood dripping from the back of his head. "Ooh dat musta hurt," said Yerkes with a New York accent. Then he let out a wicked laugh.

Wally looked at his motionless brother in fear and pleaded with Yerkes. "Come on, man! Willy needs medical attention. Please call the town's medic! Please!"

Yerkes stood on top of Willy and said, "Tell you what, scumbag! You answer a few of my questions the right way and we will see about getting your baby brother some help, okay?!"

Wally was very concerned for his brother, but had no choice but to agree. "Okay, what do you want?"

"Why did you two scumbags brutally kill that young girl?

Wally was in shock. "Girl?!" he yelled. "What fucking girl are you talking about? We didn't kill no girl!"

Yerkes smiled and made a buzzing noise. "WRONG ANSWER!" He then slammed the butt of his gun against Willy's head again.

Wally lunged at Yerkes as best as he could

with his hands tied behind his back. But he was no match for a man with a gun.

Yerkes swung his pistol toward Wally, which stopped Wally in his tracks. "Try that again, big man, and you and your brother are both dead. Now sit down on the floor! I'm not done asking my questions. And now I think you understand the importance of answering them correctly!" Yerkes said maniacally. "Now, why did you two kill and torture that young woman?"

"Deputy, please. We didn't kill anyone. Please, sir. I beg you to believe me."

Yerkes just stared at Wally for a few minutes before he narrowed his eyes and released another fury of rage onto Willy's head, this time with his night stick, while still pointing his pistol at Wally.

Wally was in disbelief. His heart sank. He yelled out, "I DID IT! I KILLED HER! WILLY HAD NOTHING TO DO WITH IT! NOW PLEASE, I BEG OF YOU, GET HIM SOME HELP!"

Yerkes looked over at the big man begging for his brother's life and said, "So you admit you strung her up and tortured her to death?"

Wally, in an emotional meltdown state, knew he had no choice but to agree in order to save his brother's life. "Yes, I killed her. I tortured her. It was me – all me. Anything you want! Just get my brother some help!"

"See, big man, that wasn't too hard. Feels good to let it all out!" Yerkes pulled a small recorder out of his pocket. "This here is my little recorder I use to record traffic stops. And now we are going to use it to record your confession. You will agree to everything and answer in a responsible manner, or I will finish bashing your brother's brains in. Understood?"

Wally nodded.

"Wally, as you know, I am Deputy Yerkes from the Top County Sheriff's Department. And I am recording our conversation because you want to openly and freely confess to the killing of the young girl we found today. Is this correct?"

"Yes, it is."

"Wally, why are you confessing to me now?"

"Because I can't handle what I've done. I'm a monster. I got my brother hurt and he had nothing to do with it."

"Wally, can you give me an account of what happened?"

"I can't remember anything. It's blank. I fucking enjoyed killing her is all I know. And all I'm ever going to say about it."

Yerkes stopped the recorder and said,

"Very well played, big man. Now you will only tell Johnson and the courts that you killed her and enjoyed it. And that there's nothing more, no matter how hard they try. Or I'll find your brother and finish off the job." With that, Yerkes landed off another blow to Willy's head. "You understand me, boy?!"

"Jesus Christ, please stop! You're killing him! I'll do whatever you say!"

"Good! Now deny that you used any type of video or camera in the killing. Got that, boy?" Yerkes said as he raised his night stick above Willy's battered, bloody head.

"Yes! I hear you loud and clear! I just don't think the sheriff will believe any of this," Wally said with a crackling voice.

"Well, big man, you best be convincing. Because if not, I'll make a complete retard out of your brother here! If he's not one already. Plus, the big bad sheriff days are numbered. His biggest mistake was coming to Top County!"

"Yerkes, why the fuck are you doing all of this? Why?"

"I'll tell you why. This town is mine, and the fucking people in it are going to respect me. I'm tired of playing second fiddle! It's my time – my town!"

"You're insane! And if I ever get the

chance, I'm going to kill you!"

Yerkes let out a wicked laugh. His eyes appeared to turn black while his face tightened and he let out another hard hit to Willy's head. Willy's body jerked from the hit, but returned motionless. "Don't ever threaten me again or I'll kill him!"

"Okay, Yerkes, you win! Please just get him some help before he dies! Because if he does, then there is nothing to stop me from telling the sheriff the truth."

Yerkes studied Wally for a second or two, reached for his cell phone, and called into the fire station to dispatch their ambulance, stat. He then instructed Wally to get into the back of his police cruiser. "Best you be nice and quiet so I can save your retarded brother."

What seemed like hours to Wally was just a few minutes. The rescue truck arrived and Simon Moreau jumped out.

Yerkes met him and said, "He's in the house, Simon." Simon noticed Wally in the backseat of Yerkes' cruiser as he began entering the house. He ran over to Willy and started taking his vitals. He turned to Yerkes and said, "What happened to him, Ben?"

Yerkes hesitated for a second and then said, "He resisted arrest, so I had to hit him with my night stick."

Simon looked up at Yerkes and asked, "How many times? His head looks like a balled-up pepperoni pizza!"

Just then, two other EMTs arrived. They all worked together to stabilize Willy enough to move him to the back of the rescue truck. They rushed him to the hospital while Yerkes brought Wally into the station.

Betty was about to leave when she heard Yerkes demand, "Open the cell, Betty! I caught the sick bastard that killed the young girl!"

Betty opened the cell and watched as Yerkes put Wally inside. She shut and locked the cell door.

Yerkes instructed Wally to bring his hands to the small opening in the door, through the slot. Wally was somber and broken, but he followed Yerkes orders. Yerkes uncuffed Wally and looked at Betty. "The sum-bitch confessed." Then he looked at Wally. "Tell her, Wally! Tell Betty what you told me."

Wally always liked Betty when he worked with her doing charity work. So he took a deep breath before saying, "I killed her."

Betty gasped and said, "Oh my!"

Yerkes closed the outer steel door to the cell and went to a desk to show Betty the tape recording. "Betty, you called it! The scumbag killed her."

Betty was still in disbelief, but managed to say, "But what about Willy?"

"Nothing to do with it! But I had to whack him over the head a few times to gain control of the situation. He's in the hospital now."

Betty grabbed for the police radio mic and exclaimed, "I'm calling Sheriff Johnson!"

Yerkes stopped her. "Betty, let the sheriff rest tonight. He's been through a lot his first few days here. Besides, Wally isn't going anywhere. So let's lock up and call it a night. I think Top County can make it through one night without the station being open. Besides, if someone needs me, you'll have the dispatch phone and you can call me."

Betty agreed and they both locked up and headed home.

Betty was almost to her home when she realized she left the dispatch phone on her desk. She turned her car around and mumbled to herself as she entered the station, "I could be in a hot bath right about now! But nooooooo, I had to forget the phone." She grabbed the phone and started to walk out before she heard, "HEY!"

Wally continued, "I need some water!"

Betty was visibly annoyed, but opened the outer steel door to the cell and pointed. "There's a water bubbler right there, Wally!"

"Betty, I know, but it's not working. I'm dying of thirst!"

Betty, not to be fooled, said, "Oh yeah? Then push the button!"

Wally pushed on the water bubbler button a few times to prove nothing was coming out.

Betty retrieved four bottles of water and handed them to Wally through the small opening of the second door. On the last bottle, Wally grabbed Betty's hand and pulled her hard through the slot. "Betty, I don't want to hurt you, but I will if you don't give me the key for this cell door."

Betty tried to maintain her composure. "Sorry, Wally, I only have the outside door key. The other one is on my desk."

Wally got angry and pulled harder. "Betty, it's the same fucking key!" He reached around Betty's tiny body and yanked the key off of her side. He unlocked the door and threw Betty in the cell.

"Please don't hurt me," Betty pleaded.

Wally looked at her, saw that she was about to piss her pants, and went to find her some blankets and towels. He returned and said, "Here, take this stuff to clean up and stay warm!" Betty was afraid to move, so Wally placed the items next to her. "Betty, I'm sorry for doing this, but everything is not what it seems. May I please have your car keys and cell phone?"

Betty's whole body was shaking, but she handed Wally the keys and the phone.

"Thank you. You will be okay until the sheriff comes in in the morning. I must go, but please try and calm down." He started out the door.

Suddenly Betty spoke up. "Wally, why?"

He stopped at the door and looked down for a few seconds, but said nothing. He left the building, got in Betty's car, and drove off.

11
UNEXPECTED VISIT

Sheriff Johnson was home doing work on his house while waiting for the email from his friend Mike Baker. *Ding!* Johnson ran over to his personal computer and read the email:

NAME: TORRINGTON DELL, JR.
ADDRESS: 1236 SKYLINE DRIVE
CITY: NEW YORK CITY
AGE: 32
OCCUPATION: PHOTOGRAPHER / FREELANCE
RECORD: CLEAN
SIDE NOTE: WENT TO HARVARD, MAJORED IN FORENSIC SCIENCE

Pat, this guy graduated at the top of his class and is squeaky clean. Let me know if you need me to dig further into the family tree.

-MIKE

Suddenly, there was a knock at Johnson's door. He looked at his watch, saw it was 9pm, and wondered who it was. He opened the door to see his friend Simon.

"Hey, Simon! What brings you out here at this time of night?"

"Pat, it's kind of an official call," answered Simon.

"Oh, okay. What's on your mind?"

Simon wasn't one to mince words. "I think your deputy is guilty of excessive force."

Johnson gave a puzzled look. "Come on in, Simon. Have a seat at the table. I'll pour coffee and you can explain this."

"You mean you don't know?" Simon replied.

"Don't know what?"

"Your deputy just about caved the skull in on Willy Smally."

"What the fuck are you talking about?"

"We got a call at the station for a medic out at the Smally house. When I got there, Wally was in the back of Yerkes' cruiser handcuffed and Willy was in the house lying face down with his hands bound behind his back with a lamp cord. Half of his skull was bashed in by your deputy!"

"Go on."

"Yerkes said Willy was resisting arrest, but the way his head was bashed in, he was clearly hit several times. After the first hit, I don't believe Willy was doing much resisting. Pat, I'm writing this up as excessive force against the Top County Sheriff's Department. And I understand you have only been on the job for a few days, so that's why I'm telling you first before I send it to the state police for review."

"Write it up if you must, but don't send it in just yet. Give me a few days to clarify things."

"Why?"

"I have a gut feeling there is way more to this than meets the eye. So I'm asking you to trust me for a few days."

"Fine, Pat, I will do what you ask. But if Willy don't make it – I'm sending it!"

"Fair enough. Do you think Willy will make it?"

"He's a tough kid, but it's hard to tell. Have to see if he makes the next few days. But even if he does, he may have brain damage. Once he's stabilized, he will be moved to Bangor General."

"Simon, make your report and put a copy on my desk tomorrow. Thanks for coming out.

I need to head to the station now and find out what the fuck is going on, and why I wasn't informed about this arrest."

"Be careful, Pat. Yerkes seems to be a bit loose."

Johnson gave his look and said, "Duly noted." He walked Simon out, got in his truck, and headed to the station. He was pissed and puzzled about not being informed about the arrest.

He arrived at the station just as the wind was starting to pick up. He stepped out of his truck and his hat was immediately taken off by a gust. This enraged him more because it was his special hat given to him as a gift and he didn't want to look silly chasing it around the parking lot. Once he retrieved it and secured it on his head, he walked into the station with a grin, remembering the person who had given him the hat.

The grin didn't last long because the station was dark – not a single light turned on. His caution intensified when he realized that the main door was unlocked. He drew his gun and flicked on the main lights. The place appeared to be completely empty. Then he heard a familiar voice coming from the entrance.

"Pat? Pat, it's me! Timber. From the diner."

Johnson walked over to her, but with his finger over his mouth. He motioned her to head his way. Then he whispered, "Tim, stay right here. I have to clear the station."

"Why, Pat? What's wrong?"

Johnson gave her his look and said with authority, "I don't know yet. Just stay here!"

Timber nodded while Johnson proceeded to check the station. He checked every room. All clear. The broom closet was a mess – like someone was looking for something – but so far, all clear. He had just one more room to check and that was the jail cell. He made his way to the outer cell door, slowly putting his hand on it to pull lightly. Then he heard someone behind him. He spun around with his gun drawn, but it was just Timber. She freaked out and screamed, which caused Betty to scream. Johnson spun back around to discover Betty locked in the holding cell.

"Jesus Christ! You girls know how to age a man! Betty, are you alright?!"

"Yes, I'm fine! Now get me the hell out of here!"

"Where's the key, Betty?"

"Wally Smally took it! But there are a few spares in the broom closet somewhere!"

"Okay, you stay here and Timber and I will go look for them."

Betty was not amused. She just muttered, "Oh, you're a riot! A real riot, Sheriff!" which made them all chuckle.

Timber followed Johnson into the broom closet. "Tim, why did you come to the station tonight?" Johnson asked.

"Well, mister tough guy, I saw you chasing your silly hat from the diner as I was closing up. And since you didn't come in today to say hi, I thought I'd come over and see if you were mad at me or something," replied Timber.

Johnson looked at her and said, "First off, it's not a silly hat. And secondly, I had a day from hell. Well, until now."

Timber smiled and handed Johnson the keys. "This what you're looking for?" she said as she swung the keys from her finger. "You know, cowboy, you're useless without me!"

Johnson gave his look, grabbed the keys, and walked over to let Betty out of the holding cell. "Betty, Wally must've took the spare keys, as well. We will have to wait till morning to get a locksmith over here," said Johnson jokingly.

Betty looked unamused. "You have Smith right there in your holster, along with Wesson! Now shoot the damn lock!"

"Betty, how did you get in here in the first place?" asked Timber.

"Wally. He tricked me. I came back for the

dispatch phone after I forgot it. He heard me and asked for water – said the bubbler was broke. I brought him a few bottles of water and he grabbed my arm through the door. I'm sure you see how that turned out."

Johnson unlocked the cell door, walked over to the water bubbler, and pulled a wad of cloth out of the spout. "Oldest trick in the book, Betty! Guess we will have to go over a few rules when we have a guest in lockup."

"Pat, be easy on her. She was just trying to be nice. You should try it sometime!"

"Tim, being nice will get you killed. Betty was very lucky tonight." Johnson turned to Betty and said, "I'm glad you're okay." He gave her a hug and asked, "Now, what is this all about? Why did Yerkes arrest Wally tonight and why was I not informed?"

"Ben didn't want to bother you tonight. He said you have been nonstop since being in town, and that the good news could wait until the morning."

"What good news?" questioned Johnson.

"Wally confessed to Ben for killing that young girl."

"What?!" said Timber and Johnson at the same time.

"It's true! Ben gave me a recording of Wally's confession to put in the evidence box.

Let me play it for you."

Betty played the recording for everyone. When it was over, both Timber and Johnson said, "Something's wrong." They looked at each other and said, "Knock it off!"

Johnson gave Timber his look and got back to business. "Betty, how did Yerkes come to get this confession?"

"He figured he would go talk to Wally and Willy just to feel them out. Then this happened. I have no idea what brought on the arrest. He said he would explain in the morning."

"Who has your car, Betty? I saw it drive away and thought it was you," Timber asked.

"Wally took it."

Johnson slammed his fist on the desk and said, "Great. Wally has a car and more-than-likely he's going to find his brother. Call the hospital and apprise security. Give them a description of Wally and have them put a guard on Willy's room. I'm going to head down there and stake out the place to see if Wally shows up. Timber, can I borrow your vehicle?"

"Sure, but why?" Timber answered.

"Because Wally knows what my truck looks like, and he may think he has a little time to plan this out. I'm sure he thinks no one knows he escaped."

"Wow, cowboy, good thinking. I'll go get

my truck and meet you out front."

Johnson turned to Betty and said, "Do not call Deputy Yerkes."

"Why not?" answered Betty.

"I can't explain it yet – just don't. Now make your call to the hospital then head home for the night. You can take my truck home and bring it back tomorrow when you come in."

"Okay, Sheriff. Be safe."

Johnson walked out of the station mumbling, "Why does everyone keep telling me that" to himself. Suddenly, he heard a rumble and saw a dark blue souped-up Scout II with big mudding tires pull up.

The window rolled down to reveal Timber. "Need a ride, cowboy?"

"Dang, nice truck! Now get out so I can go!"

"No way! I go where my truck goes."

"Tim, this is dangerous and official police business. Now out!" said Johnson with authority.

"Nuh-uh. My truck," Timber said with finality.

"Fine, have it your way. I'll just take my truck." Suddenly he heard his truck start up and drive away with Betty behind the wheel.

"Well, cowboy, it's now or never."

Johnson gave Timber his look and said,

"Slide over and I'll get in."

Timber laughed and said, "I hope so."

They arrived at the hospital and found a good out-of-the-way parking spot with clear visibility of the hospital grounds.

"You sure he will show?" asked Timber.

"Nope. Just a hunch."

They sat for a few minutes before Timber looked at Johnson and said, "I wanted to be a cop. Even took all the courses in criminal justice. I graduated second in my class. Then I got accepted into the police academy in Bangor."

Johnson kept an eye peeled for Wally, but was surprised by Timber's confession. "What happened?"

Timber got noticeably upset and stared at the hospital for a while before answering, "I don't want to talk about that right now."

One of Johnson's greatest assets throughout life was to know when to shut up. "Okay, Tim. Maybe later."

"Yeah, maybe later."

"Do you have your cell phone on you?"

"Yes. Why?"

"Let's exchange phone numbers," offered Johnson.

While they were exchanging numbers, Timber got a smirk on her face and said, "What a way to get a girl's phone number."

"Ha-ha. I want you to stay in the truck and keep your eyes focused for Wally. I'm going to scope the place out. If you see Wally, call me immediately and stay in the truck!"

"Ten-four, sir!"

Johnson gave Timber his look and got out of the truck. He headed to the back of the hospital while Timber whispered, "Be careful, cowboy" to herself.

Meanwhile, Deputy Yerkes was headed back to the station to make sure Wally was sticking to the story. Thoughts were running through his head about how he didn't get the sheriff position. He felt it should be him in charge. He started to talk to himself, "I'm the sheriff of Top County — not that outdated hick Johnson! I'll show them. I'll show them all! Sheriff Taylor didn't think I was good enough so he just had to poke his nose into my private affairs. Old man! See what happens when you cross me?" He let out a wicked laugh before saying, "You end up dead!" He had anger in his eyes. "Just had to go poking where you shouldn't have been poking, you stupid old man!"

Yerkes pulled into the station, sat in his car for a few minutes, and then started to grin. "Not now, Wally. First I think I'll go have a little visit with your dear retarded brother. Take a few pictures of my gun pressed up against his bashed-in head! Just to make sure you understand the predicament of our little agreement! Be right back, big man." He ended his self-talking with uncontrollable laughter and then headed to the hospital.

Timber was still sitting in her truck bored and listening to the radio. She thought to herself, *Hmm, a coffee would be good right about now. I'll just sneak into the hospital and grab one from the vending machine and come right back.*

She headed inside and went to the vending machine. *I better get cowboy one just in case.* She finished putting the lids on and turned around to head back to the truck.

Suddenly, she bumped into Deputy Yerkes and dropped both cups of coffee. He kicked the cups to the side and asked, "What are you doing here, Timber?"

She responded, "I'm visiting a friend!" and tried to walk around him.

He blocked her and said, "What friend? Visiting hours are over."

Timber needed to think quick. "Okay, fine. If you must know, I was visiting Dr. Ward."

"Dr. Ward? What for?" Then Yerkes smiled and said, "You slut – you're banging Ward, aren't you? I always knew you were a slut." Then he grabbed Timber by the arm and looked her in the eyes. "Leave Dr. Ward alone. He's married and I don't want a piece of trash like you fucking that up."

Timber tried to pull away, but Yerkes pulled harder and then grabbed her by the cheeks with his free hand. "Get the fuck out of here, slut. I'll deal with your skank ass later. Understood?" After Timber nodded, he said, "Good. And maybe later I'll find out just how good of a fuck you really are. Now get out of here!"

Timber pulled away and ran out of the hospital while Yerkes continued into the lobby.

Meanwhile, Johnson was in the hospital checking the side doors to make sure they were locked. A security guard met him in the hallway and said, "Evening, Sheriff."

"Evening, Sergeant. All quiet here?"

"Yes, sir. So far. But what's this all about?"

"I have a reason to believe Wally Smally may be coming for a visit. Do you have a guard on Willy Smally?"

"Yes, sir, we sure do."

"Excellent. How's the perimeter?"

"Sheriff, as you can see, everything is locked, alarms are on, and there's no way in and no way out. Except the main lobby."

Johnson looked at the sergeant and said,

"If there's a way out, there's a way in. Hence me standing here."

"Point taken. I'll go recheck the north side."

"Okay, keep a sharp eye out and make sure your radio is connected to the hospital intercom."

"Yes, sir."

"Good. If you see Wally, just let it rip over the intercom and I'll come running."

"Ten-four, Sheriff."

Meanwhile, Timber was trying to call Johnson, but all of the calls were going to voicemail. *Shit*, Timber thought, *time to put some of your training to good use. We have to find the sheriff!*

She headed to the rear of the hospital. She tried a few doors, but they were all locked. She saw a car pulling in with no headlights on, so she hid behind a dumpster and watched. She realized that it was Betty's car and her heart started to pound knowing Wally was in it. She made sure to remain very still and quiet.

She looked up at a sign that read MORGUE when suddenly a door opened up right by the dumpster. She saw Quincy Smith, who was heading home after a long day. She tried to get his attention without being seen by Wally. But he walked right by her.

Wally snuck up behind Quincy and

knocked him over the head with his fist. Quincy had no idea what hit him, but suddenly his legs buckled and he went down. Wally caught him and carried him over to Betty's car.

Timber heard him say, "Sorry, old man, but I need your keys" then saw him fumble around with the keys until he found the one that unlocked the morgue door. He swung the door open and walked in.

Timber reacted quickly. She put a soda bottle she found in the door to stop it from closing completely. She tried to call Johnson one more time, but again: nothing. *Screw it*, she thought before she headed into the morgue right behind Wally.

Meanwhile, Deputy Yerkes was attempting to walk past the security desk.

The desk officer stopped him and said, "Excuse me, Deputy, may I help you?"

"Yes, I'm going to check on Willy Smally. I was the arresting officer, and I would like to see how he's doing. Do you know which room he's in?"

"Deputy, he is in intensive care. No visitors allowed. Doctor's orders."

Yerkes looked a bit agitated and responded with authority. "It's official police business. That overrides doctor's orders."

"Sorry, not going to happen without Dr.

Ward's consent."

"Fine! Then get Ward on the phone now! They give you wannabes a tin badge and look out!"

The desk officer ignored what Yerkes said and picked up the phone to call Dr. Ward. Ward was a family man who was devoted to his wife and children. He loved the town folk and the town, as well. He was a nice man and the type of doctor everyone wished they had. One that truly cared.

"May I help you, Deputy?"

Yerkes spun around and said, "Well that was fast! I need to see Willy Smally! And rent-a-cop here says I need your permission."

"The front desk officer is correct. You do need my permission, and I'm not giving it. Willy is in a coma and cannot be disturbed."

"Doc, I don't want to disturb him. Just look in on him. Let's go over there for a minute to speak in private."

They walked to a nearby corner in the hall.

"Look, doc, I know you're banging that slut from the diner. Now let me see Willy or your wifey is going to know all about you and the whore. Let's just say your marriage will go timber."

Ward exploded. "GET OUT! GET OUT NOW, YOU SICK BASTARD! HOW DARE

YOU SAY SUCH A THING!"

Yerkes grabbed the doctor and pushed him into a wall. "Listen up, doc. I know you have been banging the little tramp. She told me so. Matter of fact, she just left here."

Dr. Ward looked Yerkes in the eyes and yelled, "YOU'RE INSANE. IF SHE WAS HERE, IT WAS NOT TO SEE ME. I SAW HER AND THE NEW SHERIFF SITTING IN THE PARKING LOT TOGETHER TONIGHT."

Yerkes tightened his grip on the doc and said, "What would Sheriff Johnson and slut-so be doing sitting in a second-rate hospital parking lot at night?"

"Maybe doing what you should be doing – looking for Wally Smally. He broke out of jail so the sheriff put the hospital on lockdown because Wally may be coming this way to see his brother."

Yerkes couldn't hide the surprised look on his face. "How do you know all this? Who told you?"

"Betty called and filled us in. Question is: why don't you, the deputy, know all this? Something's wrong here. Very wrong," said Ward. Then he started screaming, "GUARD! GUARD!"

Yerkes reacted quickly and punched Ward

in the stomach, which caused Ward to double over. Then Yerkes hit him over the back of the head with his night stick. Ward went down right before the security guard came over screaming, "HEY! WHAT'S GOING ON HERE?!"

Yerkes shouted back, "GET OVER HERE QUICK! DR. WARD JUST GRABBED HIS STOMACH AND DOUBLED OVER IN PAIN!"

The guard rushed over to Ward and was met with Yerkes' night stick right in the face. Blood splattered all over the hallway as Yerkes went into a fit of rage and began hitting the guard in the face repeatedly. His face was beaten so badly that it was unrecognizable.

Yerkes noticed the guard had a folding knife in his belt, so he removed it and opened the blade to stab the doctor five times in the heart. As if that wasn't enough, he slashed Ward's throat before dropping it and stepping back. "Oh, my! Look what that sick bastard Wally Smally did!" he laughed as he headed for intensive care to find Willy, and hopefully Wally, too.

12
RED HANDED

Wally made his way to the stairwell, which led to the lobby. He slowly looked around the hall corner into the lobby. He saw that the guard wasn't at his desk, so he made his way over to the other side of the lobby and thought about how deserted the hospital was at night. It gave him chills, but he was relieved that he hadn't been noticed so far. He made it to the outer side and turned to go down the next hallway to the nurse's station.

Suddenly, the look of horror came over his face as he stood in front of a dead Dr. Ward and the security guard. He started to freak out and became mortified at the bloody picture he was suddenly staring at. But he regained some of his composure and compassion before kneeling down to check the pulse of each man.

They were both dead, as he suspected. Fear was starting to set into him as crazy thoughts entered his head. He decided that he must continue on to Willy. *Objective: get Willy the fuck out of here*, he thought to himself.

He started to hear footsteps coming from behind him, and without thinking he picked up the bloody knife and turned around in a self-defense stance. He found himself facing Sheriff Johnson, a face that said it all. Johnson drew his gun and screamed, "DON'T FUCKING MOVE AN INCH!"

Meanwhile, Timber was spooked from being in the morgue. She thought someone was following her, so she ran up the stairwell and toward an exit sign. She used her 135lb body to body-check the door open. *WHAM!* She ran right into Sheriff Johnson, taking them both down. Johnson's gun went flying out of his hand and down the hallway. Wally used this as an opportunity. He hit the hallway lights off and ran.

Yerkes was watching the whole thing go down from the second floor guard room, where the surveillance cameras were. He was erasing the footage of him killing Dr. Ward and the security guard. Once finished, he headed out after Wally, knowing this was the golden opportunity to make himself look like a hero.

The town will praise me after I kill Wally – after all, he just killed a young girl, a security guard, and the town's beloved doctor! To top it all off, the new town sheriff is now the witness! Yerkes thought to himself.

Sheriff Johnson was laying on the ground with Timber on top of him. She looked at him, blinked twice, and said, "I just fucked something up, didn't I?"

Johnson gave her his look and pushed her off of him with just the right amount of force for her to land on her butt. He got up, retrieved his gun, and holstered it. Timber pulled his hat out from under her butt and said, "You looking for this, cowboy?" Johnson grabbed it from her, fixed it, and placed it back on his head.

"Now, tell me why you didn't stay in the truck like I said!" Johnson said with authority.

"Pat, Deputy Yerkes is here. I tried calling your cell, but it went straight to voicemail. I ran into him in the lobby and he was acting all crazy." Then Timber noticed the dead bodies in the darkened hallway. "Pat... is that Dr. Ward? Are they dead? Oh, my god! Pat! Did Wally do this?!"

"It sure looks that way," Johnson responded.

"Why would Wally do this? This is completely insane! Looks like the doctor's throat was slit, and clearly the guard's head is caved in!"

Johnson just looked at Timber and said, "Yes, it does. And you're not freaked out about this crime scene?"

"Yes, I am, but I studied forensic science at the State Police Academy, so I've seen it before."

"Come on, Tim, let's talk on the way to check on Willy. Why was Yerkes here?"

"I don't know, but I did see Wally drive up in Betty's car, so I hid behind a dumpster. Quincy Smith was leaving so Wally knocked him on the head, placed him in Betty's car, and took his keys to enter the hospital through the morgue."

"Did Wally kill Quincy?"

"No, just a love tap on the head."

Interesting, Johnson thought to himself.

Suddenly Yerkes appeared in front of them. He had a change of plans and decided to confront the sheriff. "Holy shit! Sheriff, what's going on?"

Johnson was not amused with Yerkes, but hid the feeling. "It's not good, Deputy. It looks like your escaped prisoner killed Dr. Ward and the security guard. What are you doing here?"

"If you must know, I felt bad for knocking Willy on the noggin. I couldn't sleep, so I figured I'd come check on him. I ran into Ward and he told me Wally escaped. Why did you not call to apprise me of the situation? Not very sheriff like, if I do say so myself. Instead, you take a police academy drop-out on a stakeout!"

"Puff down, Deputy-" Johnson started to say before Yerkes cut him off.

"I will not puff down! You put this whole town in jeopardy and now two people are dead so you could have a little private fling with your floosy! Oh, the great Sheriff Johnson! But don't worry – I'll help you fix your incompetence!"

Johnson walked right up to him and let it all out. "Deputy, proper police protocol for a mere deputy is to call his superior officer – ME! – and inform him of what he uncovered and to call for backup – again, ME! – before taking any action for what he may think is the victim's killer or killers. You obviously have a lack of basic police training to not inform the sheriff of a dangerous prisoner in lockup, followed by leaving the said prisoner unsupervised so you can go home and sleep because you are tired. That is a derelict of duty at the least! Protocol states no prisoner in lockup will be left unattended. NO! Deputy, you are responsible for putting the people of this town in jeopardy and are directly responsible for two people dying tonight! We will deal with the infractions later. Right now, we have a suspect on the loose and we need to find him." He poked Yerkes in the chest hard with one finger and finished by saying, "Off the record, Ben, if you ever get personal or insulting with me or the company I keep like that again, I will knock the shit out of your stupid ass! Do we understand each other?"

Yerkes was silent for a few seconds. He looked at Timber and said, "I'm really sorry, guys. I know I fucked up. I am... was upset about not getting the sheriff position, and I guess I started thinking a little stupid. Sheriff, I can learn a lot from you and I hope we can start over. Please?"

Timber remained silent. She wasn't sure where the sheriff was going with this, so she felt it was best not to say anything.

"Ben, it's forgotten. Now we got some police work to do. Go down to the lower parking lot and check on Dr. Smith. Wally clobbered him on his way in," directed Johnson.

A voice came from the hallway. It echoed. "I got a God-awful headache, Sheriff! But I'm fine!" Suddenly Quincy came walking up, continuing, "I see we have a big problem going on here. What in tarnation is happening around here? Did the sum-bitch that knocked my noggin do this to Ward and Jeff?"

Yerkes spoke up, "Yes, and he's still on the loose. It's Wally Smally!"

Quincy laughed and said, "Wally? You think Wally did this? Impossible! He is as harmless as a wingless fly." He turned to the sheriff and asked, "Is this right?"

"Sorry, Quincy, but it sure looks that way," Johnson answered.

"That sum-bitch," the coroner mumbled. "Okay, let me do my thing and clean up this mess. You go do yours."

"You need any help?" offered Johnson.

"No. I'll call in some of the staff. This is personal. Ward was a very good friend, and Jeff was a top-notch, very loyal guard, as well as a friend."

Johnson nodded. He turned to Yerkes and said, "Ben, get the other security guards together and tell them what happened. Put two guards on Willy's room. Stay here tonight. Wally may think we are both looking for him out in town, so he may come back thinking it's clear. I want a police officer here if he does."

"You bet, Sheriff! I'm on it," responded Yerkes. He started to walk away, but then stopped and turned back to say, "Timber, I'm sorry. Are we good?"

Timber nodded and smiled. "All good!"

Yerkes headed off to do his assigned task.

Timber looked at Johnson and said, "Cowboy, something doesn't feel right. Did you notice the blood drops on Yerkes' shoes?"

"I sure did, Tim. I sure did. I just didn't want to play that card yet. Come on, let's get back to the station."

"The station? With Wally still out there?" Timber asked surprised.

"He won't be doing anything more tonight except thinking. Come on, let's go!"

"Okay. I sure hope you know what you're doing."

Johnson gave his look and started walking. On the way out of the station, Johnson gave Betty a call and asked her to meet them at the station. He told her it was official business. Betty agreed to do so and they all met shortly after.

Johnson filled Betty in on everything that had happened – every single horrid detail of what unfolded. Betty was taken aback because Dr. Ward was a good friend of hers. She said, "Geez, Pat. Do you really think Wally did this?"

"I don't know, Betty. All I know is what I saw before I was clobbered by the door ram over there," Johnson said as he pointed to

Timber.

Johnson walked over to his desk and opened the top draw. He grabbed something before saying, "Now, the second reason I called you in tonight." He turned to Timber and said, "Put your right hand over your heart and listen."

"What? Why?" responded Timber.

Johnson ignored the questions and continued, "Do you, Timber Donahue, swear and solemnly agree to hold up and enforce all the laws bestowed on the Top County Sheriff's Department as a sworn law enforcement officer, and perform all the duties of a Deputy Sheriff with honor and obedience to serve and protect the public of Top County."

There was a long pause. Timber was dumbfounded, but Betty was excited and elbowed her. "Say I do, silly!"

Timber was shocked and in disbelief. This was her dream come true. Her eyes teared up, which made Betty's eyes tear up. She looked Johnson in the eyes and slowly and softly said, "I do!"

"Then by the power invested in me by the state of Maine, I duly swear in Timber Donahue as a full Deputy Sheriff of Top County with all rights and no restrictions of all law enforcement bound within the Top

County Sheriff's Department." He turned to Betty. "Betty Truman, do you swear you witnessed the swearing in of Deputy Donahue?"

"I do!" Betty said with enthusiasm.

"Deputy Donahue, please step forward." Johnson attempted to pin the badge on the newly sworn deputy.

"Ouch!" she yelled.

"Shit! Sorry, Tim!"

"Just be glad they're not silicone, cowboy!" Timber joked.

They all laughed and Timber asked, "What about my job at the diner?"

Betty jumped in. "My neighbor, Flo, is looking for a job! She used to work at Dysart's Truck Stop as a waitress!"

"Perfect, Betty! Call her and ask her if she would be interested in taking the job. If yes, Tim and I will go talk to Mr. Hammond," Johnson responded.

"Pat, I'm sure she'll take the job. She has a crush on Mr. Hammond and I believe the feeling is mutual!" Timber said as she chuckled.

"I always knew something was up with them two. Well, Betty, make it happen!" said Johnson. He turned to Timber. "Here is your police issue 45 and holster. We will all go over the specifics in the morning. Now, I think we should all go home and get some rest! I want everyone here tomorrow at 6am."

Betty winked at Timber and left.

"Pat, I want to thank you for this golden opportunity to prove myself."

"I don't want you to 'prove yourself' – just be yourself! Come on, I'll walk you to your truck!"

They walked outside just in time to see Betty drive off in Johnson's truck. "Shit," he said.

"Well, cowboy, I guess I'm giving you a ride home!"

Johnson looked at Timber and winked.

On the way to Johnson's house, Timber looked over and said, "I really want to thank you for trusting me enough to make me a deputy."

"Tim, I pulled your jacket at the state police borough. You're going to make a great deputy, I'm sure."

"What the hell is going on here? Fires, murders, a crazy deputy, a suicidal sheriff… it's fucking crazy," said Timber.

Johnson slouched in the passenger seat, put his hat over his face, and said, "Third day on the job! House is a mess. Whacked-out deputy. And four murders. Welcome home, right?"

Timber looked confused. "Four murders, Pat? Who's the fourth?"

"Sheriff Taylor – that's who."

Timber hit the brakes and screeched, "WHAT?!"

"Tomorrow, Tim, tomorrow." With that, he quickly slipped into sleep.

They arrived at the Johnson home. Timber woke Johnson up and said, "Come on, cowboy. Time to go nite-nite! Wakey-wakey!"

Johnson took his hat off of his face and said, "It's late, Tim. You coming in?"

"Why, Sheriff, are you inviting little old me into your house?"

"Yeah! It's very late and you're my ride tomorrow!"

They walked into the house and said goodnight. Johnson ended up on the couch and Timber on the bed.

13
NEW DAY

Timber and Johnson walked into the station. "Morning, Betty!" Johnson announced. "Tim and I picked up your car on the way in."

"Oh, thank you," answered Betty. "Here's your truck keys. And by the way, I love your truck! It's all go and no show!"

"Picking on my truck, Betty?" Johnson retorted.

"No, sir! Not at all. Coffee's on if you all want some."

"Yes, please!" Johnson and Timber said at the same time.

Timber pointed to Johnson and said, "Somebody forgot to get more coffee for his house!"

Betty laughed and said, "Men."

"Betty, was Flo interested in my job at the diner?" Timber asked.

Betty, while carrying two cups of coffee, got a smug look on her face. "It's all set! Flo started this morning and Mr. Hammond is one happy diner owner! He wants you to stop in later so he can congratulate you."

Yerkes walked in and interrupted, "Congratulate you for what?"

Timber turned around and proudly pointed to her badge. "I'm the new Deputy Sheriff here in town!"

Yerkes stared straight with a shocked look that he couldn't hide. Finally, he said, "Well, congrats. That's wonderful. We need another deputy around here. I hear you graduated top of your class."

Timber looked surprised. "Oh... how-"

Johnson cut her off and said, "All quiet at the hospital, Ben?"

"Yes, sir. Nothing but tears over Dr. Ward. And it looks like Willy will be out of intensive care today. Top County news showed up and started asking a lot of questions. I referred them to you, Sheriff."

"Very good, Ben. That's great news about Willy. When can I question him?"

"Not sure. In a few days, I would guess."

"I want you to hit all the places you might

think Wally will be hiding out at. If you find him, call me. Do not go after him alone. I want him alive – understood?"

"Understood. Ten-four. I'll stay in touch by radio."

"Okay, be safe."

Yerkes exited the station and went on patrol.

Johnson turned to Timber and said, "I need to qualify you for your firearm. So let's go do some shooting!" He turned to Betty. "Be a doll and handle the press."

Betty spun around in her chair and said, "And tell them what?"

"Tell them everything without telling them nothing," Johnson said with a smirk.

Betty laughed and said, "So the old razzle dazzle answer it is!"

While Timber and Johnson were driving out to the shooting range, Johnson received a phone call from the hospital. The caller was head security guard Sergeant Richards. He called to explain that his surveillance tape had been compromised. Johnson ended the call and explained everything to Timber. They both looked at each other and said, "Yerkes!"

They arrived at the shooting range. Johnson looked at Timber and said, "Well, Tim, all you gotta do is hit the target. Think you can do that?"

Timber took aim and shot her entire clip, dropped the empty shells, reloaded, and emptied the second clip. Then she put in a third clip and holstered her weapon. There was nothing left to the bullseye – it was completely shot out.

Johnson just looked at her and said, "You're qualified! Now let's go pick up Wally."

Timber gave Johnson a confused look. "Pick up Wally? Cowboy, you know where he's at?"

"I think I do. There's an old underground bunker not far from their house. I used to play in it as a kid, and I bet they found it, too. And call me 'Sheriff' or 'Pat' while on the job!"

"Underground bunker? You mean like a bomb shelter?"

"Yes, exactly."

"Cowboy, that's the perfect hiding place!"

Johnson just gave Timber his look and said, "Get in the truck!"

Johnson and Timber rolled into the Smallys' driveway and made their way toward the area where the bunker is located.

"It's been a long time, Tim, so look carefully for anything that looks disturbed."

Timber noticed some trampled flowers and whispered, "Cowboy" while pointing at them.

Johnson nodded and said, "Very good. Looks like someone was in a hurry and got careless."

They proceeded to the hidden entrance of the bunker. It looked recently used. Johnson pulled his gun and Timber followed suit. Johnson flipped the cover to the bunker, which looked similar to a propane tank cover. Then he yelled down the hole, "TOP COUNTY SHERIFF'S DEPARTMENT. WALLY, GIVE IT UP – WE KNOW YOU'RE DOWN THERE. IT'S JOHNSON. COME OUT OF THERE."

"You think he's down there?" Timber asked.

Johnson bent down over the cover and said, "You smell that? It smells like a candle was just blown out." Suddenly, Johnson was pushed from the back and fell 15 feet into the bunker, knocking him unconscious upon hitting the cement floor. The cover was slammed shut and everything went pitch black.

When Johnson started to come around, he saw that he was laying on a canvas cot. As his eyes came into focus, he saw Wally sitting at the opposite end of the bunker holding his gun. Johnson slowly sat up while holding his head.

Wally said, "Far enough, Sheriff?"

Johnson said in a woozy state, "No worries there, big fella."

"Did the mighty sheriff fall?"

"No, Wally. Pushed."

"By who?"

Johnson cleared his head and said, "Wally, I don't know. It was just me and my new deputy up there, as far as I know. I swore in Timber Donahue last night.

Wally laughed and said, "So she's in it with Yerkes then? Nothing but dirty cops up here in Top County. I take it they are back stabbing you. How's it feel to be on the losing end?"

"Wally, what are you talking about? Tell me slowly because my head still hurts."

"There is a bottle of aspirin and a bottle of water on the end table by your cot. I figured your head would hurt. You were out for over five minutes and may have a concussion." He proceeded to turn on a light.

Johnson looked around the well-stocked bunker and asked, "Expecting trouble?"

"No. My brother and I are preppers and like to stay prepared. How did you know to find me here? This bunker is well hidden."

"I played here when I was a kid. It was just an empty shelter, but we made it into a fort."

"So you're from Top County?"

"Yep. Born and raised," Johnson said

before taking six aspirins. "Wally, you wouldn't have any coffee on hand, any chance?"

Wally opened up a bag and tossed Johnson a thermos.

Johnson poured some into the cap and said, "Now, Wally, you have some explaining to do."

"Come on, Sheriff! Are you playing stupid or are you really this clueless?"

"Wally, I really have no idea what's going on here. Maybe you can shed some light for me."

Wally proceeded to tell Johnson the chain of events from the beginning. He was very articulate and gave great detail. Finally, he said, "Now, we are both sitting in a bomb shelter together, except I have the upper hand!" while waving Johnson's gun.

Johnson took a while to process Wally's story. Then he said, "The hell you do! Whoever locked us in here has the upper hand!"

Wally turned a bit grey and said, "For now. But I made another way out. I will find and kill Yerkes!"

"And me?"

"You will stay in here until I kill Yerkes and get my brother. And when we are far, far away, I will call Betty and tell her where you are. Don't worry, Sheriff. There is enough supplies down here to last a year."

"Would you believe me if I told you I have nothing to do with what Yerkes did? I'm not a crooked cop, as you put it. I can help you with all of this."

Wally got agitated and said, "Help me?! That's a laugh! This is the second time you told me that, and look where me and my brother are at! My brother got his skull cracked, and I'm wanted for three murders that I didn't commit. No, Sheriff, you stay here and I will go alone. And if you're really not crooked, you will clear us by telling our story!"

"If you kill Yerkes — assuming you could — you're just as guilty as he is for taking your outlaw justice."

"Justice?! Justice?!!! You call this fucking justice? Fuck you, Sheriff. I have seen the cop's justice, so I'll take my chances and do it my way!"

"Okay, Wally, do it your way. Nothing I can do about it." Johnson poured another steaming hot coffee. In a split second, he threw it in Wally's face.

Wally screamed out in pain and put both of his hands over his face. By the time he could wipe his eyes, Johnson was on him. *Wham!* Wally was rocked in the jaw by Johnson's left hand, followed by his right. The big man fell to the ground and Johnson grabbed his gun. He holstered it and sat back down on his cot.

Meanwhile, Timber was slowly waking up from a chloroform dose. Her head was pounding, but her eyes were starting to adjust to the sunlight coming through a curded-up window. Her hands were tied high above her head and her wrists were hurting bad from her hanging body weight. She stood up on her feet to take some weight off of her wrists and regain her composure. She looked around and found herself in an old, beat-up cabin. Her hands were secured to a ceiling beam and a movie camera was straight in front of her, with two others on each side of her. A TV monitor was above the main camera. Hanging on the wall were various whips, floggers, and canes. She also noticed a cart with different types of medical surgical equipment: clamps, scalpels, scissors, and a car battery hooked up to some kind of shock probes. She knew she was in trouble. Big trouble.

A voice lit up a speaker and was electronically altered. "Hello, Timber."

She looked around the room.

"Timber, I assure you, you are alone at the moment. Except for me. And I'm quite a distance from you."

Timber strained her bindings and said,

"What do you want from me?"

"Oh, my little darling, we are going to play a game. A game that over a hundred sick perverts from all over the world will be watching. You see, little darling, they pay me large sums of money to watch pretty little sluts like yourself get tortured to death – slowly and painfully. I'm particularly going to enjoy this one, you fucking bitch. Bye, bye for now!"

Timber started to think, *I know that voice. Even though it was altered, I know that voice.* She once again frantically tried to get out of her bindings, but only ended up hurting her wrists more.

"Okay, Timber, calm down and think," she said to herself. "First day on the job and I'm more than likely going to die. What the fuck. Think of something!"

Suddenly, a figure came in the darkened room wearing all black and donning a rubber Halloween mask. It looked like a goblin with large crooked teeth and small horns on each side of the forehead.

The figure stood there looking at Timber. Being a smartass, Timber asked, "Does it speak?"

"Hello, Timber. Glad to see you're still hanging around," he said before breaking out into wicked laughter. "You will call me

Goblin." He turned on the monitor and all three cameras.

"No, I think I'll just call you dickhead!" Timber replied back.

He walked over to Timber and grabbed her hair from behind her head, forcing her to look up at the monitor. "See, bitch, you're on TV. Hope you like how you look. Because soon enough, you won't." He then punched her in the side of the rib cage. "And you will call me Goblin when spoken to. Do we understand each other NOW?"

Timber, fighting to regain her breath, gave an affirmative nod.

"See, slut, that wasn't hard. Now what's my name?"

Timber looked the man right in the face and said, "What? You don't know?"

Not amused, he grabbed Timber by the breasts and squeezed hard with a slight twisting motion.

Timber pulled back and snipped out, "Probably the best tits you ever touched!"

He slapped her across the face and laughed. Then he walked out of the room, shutting the door behind him.

The speaker came on again. "Bitch, I'm going to explain our little game to you now."

Timber only laughed and said, "I'm

listening, little boy!"

"You're tough now, bitch, but we shall see how long that lasts! Now onto the game! We have over one hundred very wealthy sick fucks from all over the world. They bid on the torture methods we are going to use on you. So when I hold up the whip, the highest bidder gets to dictate where on your body you are to be whipped. Each device has a five minute time limit, so not to have you expire too soon. This will go on with each device. Rest assured, it will be slow and painful and at some point, you will beg me to kill you. But we won't until your body decides to expire. Your job is to just hang there and suffer for the players' amusement. And if you must know, most bitches last no more than three hours. But I'm going to add a little excitement with you. I'm going to humiliate you, as well, in front of the players. This is new to the way we play the game. So you're our test pig. Any questions, bitch?"

"Yes, you sick fuck. Who the fuck are you?"

"You will know soon enough. Bye for now!"

Timber yelled, "WAIT!"

"What is it?"

"When Sheriff Johnson finds you, you're a dead man!"

The voice broke out in a hearty laugh. "Pat is going to die a slow death in that bomb shelter. You see, we plugged all the air and ventilation shaft holes."

Timber heard a click and the speaker went off.

14
THE SEARCH

Wally began to stir. Johnson, who was enjoying his coffee, said, "Welcome back."

"Fuck you, Sheriff! Why don't you just kill me and get it over with?"

"Two reasons, Wally. One, I need your help to get out of here. And two, I believe your story!"

"Sure. You're just saying that so I can get you out of here."

"No, Wally, I do believe you! But if you want to get Yerkes and whoever else is behind your setup, you must trust me and do it my way."

Wally started to cry. "I want to trust you. I really do. I'm just confused on who to trust anymore. Seems like nothing but corrupt cops everywhere."

Johnson softened his voice and said, "Wally, look at me." He lifted his left pant leg above his boots.

Wally was shocked. "Holy shit – you had a backup gun this whole time?"

"That's right. I could have taken you out at any time I wanted to. Now it's time to work together. Let's get the fuck out of here."

"Okay, come on." Wally moved a rack of shelves that exposed a small corridor. "This goes to the basement of my house."

"Well, let's go, boy!"

They exited the bunker and entered Wally's house. Wally showed Johnson the bloodstained rope that Yerkes used as his motive to bust him and his brother. "See, this is the rope. The blood is from a coyote that killed a few of our chickens."

"I believe you, Wally. Now I have to make a plan. Time is limited." Johnson pulled out his cell phone and dialed a number. "Sneaker, it's Johnson. I need your help. I'm at the Smally house. Meet me here ASAP!"

"Okay, Pat, I'm on my way. What's going on?" Sneaker responded.

"I'll tell you when you get here." Johnson then turned to Wally. "Get a few things you need – you're going into temporary hiding."

"No way! I'm in on this!"

"Wally, I need to get a handle on what's going on. If what I'm thinking is right, you would not survive a day on your own."

Suddenly, Sneaker's truck came rolling into the driveway. He jumped out and said, "Holy shit, Pat, it's all over the radio that Wally killed three people: that pour girl, Dr. Ward, and a security guard at the hospital!"

"Sneaker, there have been four murders and Wally isn't responsible for any of them. He's been set up and I need to find out why. I need you to hide Wally for a while until I can get a handle on this mess."

"You got it. Will you be in touch?"

"I will. Don't let this knucklehead do anything stupid."

Wally chimed in, "Sheriff, I want my brother!"

"I will check on him first chance I get. I promise. Now go with Sneaker. And for Pete's sake, listen to him! It just might save your life."

"Okay, I will try."

Johnson gave his look and turned to Sneaker. "Get going and stay away from Yerkes. He's crooked and dangerous. If you hear anything about Timber, call me pronto."

"Timber is missing?" Sneaker asked.

"Looks that way. Now get going! I got work to do. Keep Wally out of sight."

Sneaker looked at Wally while he was getting in his truck.

"What?" Wally asked.

"What are you doing?" Sneaker asked back.

"Um... I'm getting in your truck."

"No, Wally, you can't be seen as a lackadaisical passenger sitting in my tow truck." Sneaker opened up a side compartment. "Crawl in and hang on, kid!"

Wally looked at the compartment and said, "You got to be kidding me!" He saw the look on Sneaker's face and said, "Nope, you're not" while climbing in.

Johnson called Betty at the station, but pushed *67 before the call in order to keep the it unknown.

"Top County Sheriff's Department – Betty speaking," Betty said on the other line. "May I help you?"

"Betty, it's Johnson. Say nothing and listen. Do not call me by my name – just 'yes' and 'no' answers. Understood?"

"Yes, go ahead, caller."

"Is Yerkes or Timber in the office?"

"No, sir."

"Betty, the office may be bugged. Yerkes is responsible for killing Dr. Ward and the security guard, and quite possibly the young girl in the woods."

Betty said nothing and acted like nothing was wrong to continue the rouse.

"I will explain later. Text my phone if either of them show up."

"Yes, caller. You might want to call animal control to assist you with your cat in the tree. Their number is 564-2222."

"Betty, you deserve a big kiss! Talk soon. Bye, bye."

"Good luck with your cat!" Betty said before hanging up.

Johnson heard a crackle come over his police radio. "It's Sneaker on tact four!" Sneaker said excitedly. "I drove by the hospital and there sat Yerkes in his patrol car!"

Johnson grabbed his mic and said, "Sneaker, get the hell out of there! If Wally sees that, we got more problems! I'm on my way. And good job, Sneaker."

"Be careful, Pat!"

Johnson hopped in his truck and put the wind behind him. He raced toward the hospital. As he pulled up, he saw Yerkes' empty patrol car. Johnson parked in front of it so the car would be stuck, and proceeded to rush into the hospital straight to Willy's room.

Willy was out cold, but still alive. Johnson thought to himself, *Why is there no guard on Willy?* He went by the main desk and asked, "Is

Deputy Yerkes here?"

"Yes, Sheriff. He's in the morgue."

"Great. Do you know if he's alone?"

"Well, he went in alone, but I believe he's meeting with the coroner."

"Thanks. Why is there no guard on Willy Smally's room?"

"Deputy Yerkes said the threat was over and dismissed the order."

Johnson looked at his name tag. "Mr. Miller, I suggest you get a guard back on Willy's room, pronto! And never dismiss one of my orders unless it's from me! Understood?"

"Yes, sir. I'll take care of it right now."

Johnson headed to the morgue. He walked right in to see Yerkes talking with Quincy. "Deputy, Quincy. What do we have here?"

They both turned and Yerkes said, "Sheriff! Erm, I was just getting the coroner's report on the two hospital victims."

Johnson noticed Yerkes' little stutter.

Quincy said, "Sheriff, it's not finished yet, but it looks like the cause of death is from stab wounds."

Johnson was clearly agitated and came back with, "Yeah, no shit, Quincy. Tell me something I don't know. But for now we have another problem."

"And what might that be?" asked Yerkes.

"Well, Timber and I were at the Smally house looking down an old bomb shelter shaft when she pushed me in and locked the cover. Now she's missing."

Yerkes seized the opportunity and said, "Holy shit, Sheriff, are you okay?"

"Yes, I'm fine. I knew a secret passageway to get out from playing there as a kid."

"Was Wally there?" asked Yerkes.

"No, Deputy. No Wally."

"Do you want me to check you out?" asked Quincy.

"No, I'm fine. Thanks though." Johnson turned to Yerkes. "We have to go find Wally and Timber. They may be in this together."

"What do you want me to do?"

"Go on patrol and look everywhere. And I mean everywhere. Call me if you see anything at all. Be careful – they are dangerous."

Yerkes nodded and headed out on patrol. Johnson turned to Quincy and said, "Get me that coroner's report, stat!"

"Sure, but you can't rush these things, you know!"

Johnson gave his look and left. He called his friend Simon and said, "It's Pat. I need your help."

"What's up, Pat?" Simon answered.

"I need you and your men to go out

scouting for potential fire risks. That's the cover, but what I really need you to do is be on the lookout for Deputy Yerkes and his patrol car. Report directly back to me on his whereabouts. Call in all the men you can and flood the area. Do not approach him – just watch from a distance."

"Will do, Pat. But why?"

"Let's just say your hunch about him is coming to light. Talk to you later. Oh, and talk on the radio with your men like normal so he doesn't get suspicious."

"Will do. Be careful."

"Yeah, I know. Everyone keeps telling me that."

Johnson dialed Sneaker and asked, "How's Wally doing?"

"He is pacing more than a hungry caged cougar."

"Okay, put him on."

Wally got on the phone and immediately asked, "Is my brother okay?"

"Yes, Wally. I just saw him and he is resting comfortably. His room is guarded."

Wally gave a big sigh of relief and thanked Johnson.

"Stay put and I'll call back later."

Suddenly, Johnson saw the black Mustang slowly drive by. He jumped in his truck, hit the lights, and pulled the car over.

Johnson walked over to the Mustang and tapped on the dark-tinted window with the tip of his gun. The window rolled down and the driver said, "Can I help you, officer?" The man looked almost childlike and appeared tall and skinny.

"License and registration."

The man complied. He handed Johnson the documents. Johnson read the license and said, "Torrington Dell, Jr. from New York. What are you doing way up here?"

"Free country, officer. I'm just smelling the pine trees. And may be interested in buying out here."

Johnson looked him straight in the eyes and asked, "Is that a fact?"

"Why did you pull me over, officer?"

"It's Sheriff, boy. Your exhaust seems a bit loud and I need to check it on my decibel meter."

"You're fucking kidding, right?"

"No, son, I'm not." Johnson went back to his truck and grabbed the electrical meter he was using at his house to test the wiring. He stuck a probe in the Mustang's exhaust. "Okay, bring it up to 3,000rpms for a few seconds."

After the fake test, Johnson told him, "You're all set. It's below, so you're free to go on your way. Welcome to Top County." He turned to walk away, but stopped and turned back around. "One more thing. What does your license plate mean?"

"Just the first letters of all my best friends."

Johnson laughed and said, "That's funny. Drive safe and have a good day!"

Johnson sat in his truck sipping his coffee. He flicked on a switch from his dash, which opened a compartment to reveal a touch screen. He turned the screen on and a green blip showed up. "There you are, Mr. Torrington Dell, Jr." Johnson said to himself. "Now let's see where you bring me."

Johnson had secretly placed a tracking device on the black Mustang when he pretended to check the exhaust. He only had one tracking device and was originally going to put it on Yerkes' patrol car. But he had a hunch the black Mustang would show up eventually. He knew it would pay off.

Johnson received a text that said, "It's Simon. Yerkes is at his house. Please advise."

"Simon, watch him from a distance. Better to have a volunteer member watch so Yerkes will not recognize you."

"Ten-four," Simon responded.

Johnson drove back to the Smally house because something didn't feel right. He started poking around the entrance of the bunker. He knew he was missing something. "How did Timber leave here? My truck was left untouched," he said aloud.

Johnson walked backwards from the bunker. After about 30 feet, he stopped and studied the ground. He noticed marks on the grass. "SHIT!" he said. "She was dragged out of here! Them are heel marks!" He followed the marks to a second driveway, which was out of sight from the first one. Then he spotted a white handkerchief on the ground. He picked it up with his pen and smelled it. "Fuck – it's chloroform. She was knocked out!" He walked slowly back to the heel marks and found Timber's truck keys on the ground close to the bunker's entrance. "Okay, Timber, I got your message. Now to find you." He knew she was in big trouble.

Timber heard a vehicle pull up. Her senses were heightened because of how scared she was – scared of the unknown. She listened carefully and noticed there were two different sounding footsteps.

The man known as Goblin came through the door and said, "Oh my! The little bitch's wrists are getting bloody from the rope! What a beautiful sight!" He gave a sick laugh.

"LET ME GO!" yelled Timber. "I'M A

POLICE OFFICER AND THEY WILL HUNT YOU DOWN UNTIL THEY FIND YOUR UGLY ASS!"

Goblin strode over to Timber and punched her in the gut, knocking the wind out of her. "Shut the fuck up, bitch! Speak when spoken to and not before! And address me as 'Sir Goblin.'"

The voice that Timber heard before came over the speaker. "Goblin, do not mark her yet. You know how our guests want a fresh, unbruised body."

"I owe this bitch a little lesson!" Goblin responded.

"Unbutton her shirt."

"Yes, sir."

"Not bad looking for an older slut, would you say, Goblin?"

"Not bad at all, sir."

"Now, I want this bitch to suffer. I want you to break a few of her ribs just in the right spots, as to not bruise her. This way she'll be in severe pain, but our clients will be none the wiser. Even a light flogging will be excruciatingly painful, making her breath harder and harder until she expires. Goblin, anytime you're ready."

Goblin picked up a solid rubber mallet off the tray. He lightly held it against Timber's ribs.

"Are you ready?" he asked her.

Timber, being a wise-ass and knowing that begging was not going to help, said, "Give it your best shot, Master Fucktard!"

He swung with precision at the left side of her ribcage. The mallet made contact and two ribs cracked. Timber screamed in pain and her body jerked against her bindings.

The voice came back on and said, "Now the right side, Goblin."

"With pleasure, sir!" He raised the mallet and landed a blow to the right side of Timber's ribcage. Two more ribs broken. The cracking was muffled by her screams.

Timber shook violently, but Goblin held her still and gave her a shot that relaxed her. She was in severe pain and fighting to breathe. Goblin rebuttoned her shirt, kissed her on the lips, and left.

She tried to focus on the voice to get her mind off of the pain. *I know that voice*, she thought to herself. *Think, Timber, think.* Then she looked directly into the camera and said, "I know who you are."

The voice came on and responded, "You do, do you? And who might I be?"

In a soft but strong voice, Timber exclaimed, "You're that sexist filthy dirtbag, Joe Gordon! You are scum and a worm. You hide your shortcomings by playing cop. How you ever became the Commander of the State Police, I will never know! So how many other cadets have you raped and destroyed?"

The voice came back no longer altered. "Very good, bitch. Yes, it's me, Commander Gordon. I'm glad I made an impression on you. I'll bet you can still feel me inside of you. I know you enjoyed it – our little rape session. Nasty sluts like you just beg for it!"

Timber continued to focus on the camera and said, "You're a sick bastard and I'm going to kill you."

Gordon laughed.

Suddenly, Timber felt a tingle in her feet. Her body started to shake and twist. She was being shocked by high voltage going through the metal plate she was standing on. Once the shocking stopped, Timber's body went limp with all of her weight on her wrists. She forced herself to stand in order to relieve the pressure on her wrists.

"Bitch, be fair warned that I can kill you from Bangor if I choose. Be very careful what you say to me from now on! Say 'Yes, sir' or you will get a longer dose of electricity!"

Timber mumbled, "Yes, sir."

15
YERKES' HOUSE

Johnson checked on the location of the black Mustang. It was still sitting at Grub & Stuff. He decided that enough was enough – he headed to Deputy Yerkes' house to confront him. He spotted two firemen watching Yerkes' house. He pulled up and asked them if Yerkes was in the house.

"Yes, Sheriff. He never came out. What's this all about anyways? We're not too happy about spying on a buddy."

"I'm not sure, guys. But let's hope for the best. I owe you guys one, but I'll take it from here."

The firemen drove off and Johnson pulled into Yerkes' driveway. It was a small, one-bedroom house on a fairly busy street. The house was well-kept. Johnson knocked on the front door and gave a friendly yell. "BEN! IT'S PAT. ARE YOU IN THERE?"

There was no answer and the door was locked. Johnson knocked twice more and nothing. Johnson rubbed his hand over the top of the door frame and found the key. He laughed and thought, *This would only happen in a Jamie Santamore horror film.*

He unlocked the front door and went inside. He called out, "BEN! YOU IN HERE? IT'S SHERIFF JOHNSON." There was no answer. He looked around and everything appeared to be in place. He decided to poke around. He found a bunch of DVDs, each one marked with a number – one to nine. *Kind of odd.* There was also a lot of bondage and rape porn videos. Johnson checked inside the DVD player. He found there was already a disc inside, so he decided to hit play.

It was a video of the young girl the hikers found being tortured by a man with a mask on. He ejected the DVD and saw that it was numbered "10". He grabbed the "1" DVD, hoping it was the same girl on the disc. He popped it in the player and saw another young female victim being tortured by the same man in a mask. It looked like a goblin mask. He studied it and concluded that it wasn't Yerkes in the mask because he was too thin and tall.

And it didn't appear to be Torrington Dell, Jr. either.

Johnson packed up the DVDs and tried to open a wooden roll top desk, but it was locked. "Fuck it," Johnson said aloud before punching the wooden slats to pieces. There sat stacks of one hundred dollar bills. Johnson ran his fingers over them and figured there must be close to $500,000 in cash. He rumbled through the rest of the desk and found a letter addressed to the State Police Headquarters in Bangor from his friend Sheriff Taylor. The letter was addressed to Commander Gordon. It read:

Joe, old friend,

This is Sheriff Andrew Taylor. I need your help on the QT. My deputy, Ben Yerkes, seems to be involved with something not good. I found a bag in his patrol car with $50,000 in it. I left it in his car as to not let him know I found it. Not sure how he obtained it. Also, I seen him talking to a man in a black Mustang who checked out to be Torrington Dell, Jr. from New York. He's the son of Torrington Dell, who I busted 10 years ago in New Mexico.

Joe, I need you to get me a federal background check on Yerkes without going through the database. I don't trust anyone but you here in Top County. That's why I sent this to your private marshal fax. Please send

info back to my private fax. Thanks, Joe.
- Sheriff Andrew Taylor

Johnson looked at the sent number and recognized it. "Gordon's!" He looked back at the date the fax was sent. He checked Yerkes fax machine memory and BINGO! It was sent directly from Gordon to Yerkes. "So they must be in it together."

Johnson started thinking more dark about the entire situation. He called Betty on his cell phone.

"Top County Sheriff's Department! Betty speaking," Betty said.

"It's me. Are you alone?"

"Yes, Pat."

"In exactly 15 minutes, I want you to get on the radio and call me and Yerkes to the corner of Old Mill Road and Sebec Street. Say that there's a report of the body of a deceased woman. When I respond, say that a few campers out for a hike came across the body and that they are waiting to meet us there. And Betty, be very convincing."

"Sheriff, I'd ask why, but I already know you will say, 'Talk later.'"

"Talk later, Betty," Johnson said as he ended the call.

Meanwhile, Timber was thinking on a way

to bide the time. She came up with an idea, but it was a long shot, at best. She figured she didn't have much to lose at this point. She convinced herself that Johnson would eventually find her if she bided enough time. She refused to believe that an old bunker would be his demise. So she gathered all of her strength in order to not come across as weak.

"Hey, pussy behind the camera! You done jerking off? I want to talk to you!"

Zap! The metal plates under her feet were once again electrified. Timber's body jumped from the high voltage – body shaking and quivering from the intense pain. It felt like it went on for several minutes even though it was less than 10 seconds. It stopped and she fell limp with full body weight on her wrists. Her hands started to turn blue from the lack of circulation, and she struggled to get to her feet.

Gordon responded, "Shocking, isn't it, little bitch? What do you want, slut?"

Timber gained as much strength as she could muster, looked straight into the camera, and said, "Are you such a little man that you have to get somebody else to do your dirty work for you? Or are you too afraid to do it yourself? I mean, you asked how it felt when you were inside of me." Timber started to laugh. "To tell you the truth, I couldn't feel a thing. You're pathetic in that department. So now I know why you have to drug your women – it's because you're worthless as a man and can't get it any other way!"

Suddenly, there was a loud crack and the plates under her feet lit up. Her body started jerking much more violently than before. Gordon was losing all rationality and turned the voltage to the max. Timber was screaming in pain. Her body went limp again. Gordon regained his composure and cut the power to the plates. He realized that Timber was not worth anything dead. He thought to himself, *Being a cop, she will bring more sick players into the game, which means more money – tons more. Most of these players are extremely wealthy criminals who have a grave dislike for cops and really enjoy seeing a beautiful female cop being tortured to death slowly.*

Timber started to come around just as Goblin walked into the room. "Sir, when would you like to start the game?"

"Goblin, there is going to be a small change in plans. I'm coming up to Top County to help play this game. And I'm going to enjoy this one. I'm flying there, so meet me at the pad in two hours. Cut her down and lock her on the rack, but allow her hands to recover. I don't want her to give up too soon while playing the game."

"Yes, sir. I will be at the pad in two hours." Goblin turned the camera off.

Timber strained to get to her feet and Goblin got behind her and firmly grabbed her breasts under her shirt. He pinched both nipples hard, which woke Timber up.

"You know what, bitch? Maybe I'll fuck you before the boss gets here!" Goblin said as he slid his hand down the inside of Timber's pants.

She squirmed around and yelled out, "Yeah, go ahead! Be interested to see what Gordon does to you when I tell him you just fucked what he was flying in to do!"

"Bitch!" was all Timber heard before she lost consciousness. She woke up in a darkened room on a wooden rack with her hands and feet securely bound by shackles screwed into the wood planks.

Meanwhile, Deputy Yerkes received the call from Betty over the radio. He didn't answer it right away, wondering if he was being set up by his cohorts for the killing he did in the hospital that brought attention to the town. *Or is there really a dead woman? What if Goblin is killing them on the side.* Yerkes had a lot of thoughts going around in his head. He was clueless and didn't know what to do. So he did what he was told never to do and called

Commander Gordon's cell phone.

"Gordon here!" Gordon said.

"Joe, it's Ben. I know I'm not supposed to call you, but it's an emergency."

"It better be!" Gordon yelled. "What is it?"

Yerkes explained the radio message from Betty.

Gordon lashed out. "YOU FUCKING MORON! DID YOU EVER THINK THAT THERE WAS REALLY A DEAD BODY? JUST A COINCIDENCE? BECAUSE I ASSURE YOU IT'S NOT ONE OF OUR GIRLS. RESPOND TO THE CALL NOW, YOU DUMBASS. AND REPORT BACK TO ME LATER! I'M CURIOUS TO KNOW HOW JOHNSON ESCAPED YOUR SO-CALLED INESCAPABLE BOMB SHELTER. AND YOU'RE SURE JOHNSON HAS NO CLUE YOU PUSHED HIM DOWN THE SHAFT OR WHAT HAPPENED IN THE HOSPITAL?"

"Yes! He thinks Wally Smally did the killings at the hospital! He told me Timber pushed him down the shaft and that Wally and her are together."

Gordon laughed at the thought and responded, "Good! Now go do police work, dumbass! I'm on my way to the old landing pad at Grizzle's Old Log Yard. I'm going to help torture that bitch. Don't ask why! After this, we are going to lay low for a while. Until things quiet down."

"Yes, sir. But Joe, I want to be there to see Timber suffer. The little whore never liked me and I want to help."

Gordon laughed and replied, "Well, it looks like she has a good side after all. If everything is legit with Johnson, then meet us at the cabin. If it doesn't smell right, call me immediately" before hanging up.

Yerkes responded to Betty's call and said, "Yerkes here! Betty, I'm en route. Sorry for the delay – I was dealing with a traffic stop. I sent them on their way."

"Ten-four, Ben."

The radio cut back in with Johnson saying, "Ben, it's Johnson. It looks like a slip and fall. I'll meet you by my truck in a few minutes."

"Ten-four, Sheriff," Yerkes responded. "I'll be there in less than five minutes." Yerkes gave a sigh of relief. *A slip and fall sounds plausible in that area. There are a lot of loose rocks and unstable hiking trails.* He hit the siren and gave it hell to get the scene.

Johnson got a call from his friend, Mike Baker. "Pat, your deputy did exactly what you said he would do. Call the head cheese!"

"Excellent, Mike! Listen, it's not good at

all. It's Gordon! I had a feeling he was involved! I haven't much time, so keep this hush for now. Get your ass up here – I may need your help!"

"On my way, Pat!"

"Great, but do not call me. I will call you. Just get here and wait at the station."

"Will do. Be careful," ended Mike.

Johnson called Timber, but it went straight to voicemail.

Timber heard her phone ring with the ringtone she set for Johnson. *Save a horse, ride a cowboy! He's alive!* she thought to herself.

Goblin came into the room and picked up her cell phone. "Bitch, who is 'Cowboy?'"

Timber remained silent. Goblin pushed on Timber's broken ribs to make her scream out in pain. "It's my boyfriend!"

"See, slut, that was easy now, wasn't it? Next questions: does 'Cowboy' have a name?"

Timber was frustrated and in extreme pain, so she screamed out, "SHERIFF PATRICK JOHNSON! WHO IS, NO DOUBT, HUNTING YOU DOWN!"

Goblin laughed and said, "Oh, sweetheart. Your precious sheriff will be dead long before he gets a chance to save you. You see, corruption runs so deep that it includes some of the most powerful people in the world." He slapped her across the face and said, "See you in a little while."

Johnson heard Yerkes' patrol car siren blasting closer and closer. He poured a cup of coffee and leaned against the front of his truck. "It's showtime," he mumbled under his breath.

Yerkes pulled up, got out, and said, "Sheriff, I got here as quick as I could!"

"No problem, Ben. The body isn't going anywhere. Want some coffee? It's about a mile in."

"No, I'm good."

"Then let's get in there to process the scene! Ben, grab the camera off of my seat rest."

When Yerkes reached in Johnson's truck, Johnson threw his cell phone in the back of Yerkes' patrol car.

They walked into the woods to a small clearing. Johnson turned to Yerkes and handed him a letter.

"What is this?" Yerkes asked.

"Just read it."

But Yerkes already knew what it was. He pulled his gun on Johnson and asked, "Where did you get this?"

"I found the fax in your house along with a bunch of nice tapes and a lot of cash. I want in."

Yerkes was clearly agitated at the thought of his home being invaded. "Want in? What? Have you any idea what you stepped into?"

"No, Ben, I don't. But I like money. And I'm sick and tired of working for nothing."

Yerkes walked around Johnson to position Johnson's back to a steep drop-off. "So, tell me – where is my money?"

"It's in a safe place for now."

"You should have stayed away from Top County. Now you're going to die just like all of the others! You just had to meddle like Sheriff Taylor did."

"You killed him, Ben?"

"Yes, I killed the old geezer. And it was actually fun! But it's going to be more fun killing you. And a blast watching Timber be tortured to death! See, Sheriff, you're going to die quickly, but your precious deputy is going to suffer a slow and painful death. It'll be humiliating! Something I'm going to sure enjoy."

"Ben, how does Torrington Dell, Jr. fit into all of this? Did he recruit you or was it Gordon? Gordon promise you something you could never get on your own?"

"You know how to push buttons, don't you! Dell is a spectator! Gordon promised me money and the sheriff position you now hold.

Anyways, I have to go now. I have a torture session to watch, and three more people to kill. You know, I need to tie up some loose ends. Sheriff, don't you know you should always wear your bulletproof vest? Not leave it in your truck! Now where is my $500,000?"

Johnson gave Yerkes his look.

"Never mind. I'll find it. Bye, bye!" *BLAM! BLAM! BLAM!* Yerkes fired three shots to Johnson's chest. The closeness of the range knocked Johnson back off the twenty-foot drop-off. Johnson's body hit the ground below. Yerkes took a few pictures of Johnson's lifeless body and laughed. "Something to show your girlfriend before we kill her," he said to himself.

He got in his patrol car and sped off. He called Joe and said, "Johnson was onto us. I had to kill him."

"You killed Johnson?!"

"Yes, sir. I did. He was onto us, but had little info."

"Wait, are you telling me a moron like yourself killed Johnson? I can't believe it!"

"Believe it, sir. I have the pictures to prove it. It was rea-"

"Shut up, you idiot! You can tell me more in person. Any loose ends?" Joe interrupted.

"Yes, sir, there is."

"Then go tie them up and meet us at the cabin! I assume it shouldn't take you long."

"No, sir. Nothing to it! Be there soon!"

"Okay, Ben. You did good on killing Johnson. Don't fuck this up!"

Gordon was baffled by the fact that Johnson was sloppy enough to let a moron like Yerkes get the drop on him. But then again, Yerkes was able to get the drop on Sheriff Taylor, as well. *Maybe Yerkes has some future use,* thought Gordon.

Yerkes pulled into the station and walked in. "Betty, you here?" Yerkes looked at the clock and saw that it wasn't quite 4:30pm. *She should still be here*, he thought to himself.

The town clerk walked by the door. Yerkes asked her, "Mrs. Finn, do you know where Betty is?"

"She told me she was on an errand and would see me tomorrow," Mrs. Finn responded.

"Did she say where or what errand she was on?"

"No, Deputy, I'm sorry but she didn't."

"Thank you, Mrs. Finn."

Yerkes called Betty on her phone.

Betty saw the caller ID and decided to answer. "Hello, Ben."

"Hi, Betty! Are you coming back to the

office?"

"Ben, didn't Johnson tell you? I'm off to Portland to visit my sick sister! I won't be back until late tomorrow night. Why are you not with the sheriff on the call?"

"I came back to the station for evidence bags. Do you know where they are?"

"Broom closet, third shelf down. There should be a box of them."

"Okay, I see them. Have a safe trip. Enjoy your visit with your sister! See you later, Betty."

Yerkes decided that her death could wait a day or two. After all, she has no idea it's coming. He swung by the hospital to see if he could get to Willy. However, Willy was discharged and moved to Bangor General. *Fuck! Gordon is not going to like this! But I'm dying to see Timber tortured, so fuck it! I'm heading to the cabin!*

16
NEW GAME PIECE

Yerkes drove out to the old cabin and came across a young girl with her thumb in the air. Her name was Brandy and she was a 19 year old college student that Yerkes was acquainted with from a noise-related call when she threw a party with underage drinking. He stopped his patrol car and asked, "Where you heading, Brandy?"

"Hi, Deputy. I'm heading over to my friend Sara's," Brandy answered.

"Sara Bradly?"

"Yep, that's her, Deputy."

"Just call me Ben. Hop in – I'm going that way."

"Really? Thanks, Dep- I mean, Ben." Brandy hopped in the patrol car.

They started driving. Yerkes had a difficult

time controlling himself. He was sitting next to a young and beautiful 5'4" 118lb Mulatto woman with very short, white shorts, a beautiful skin tone, a belly chain around her waist, and a bikini top covered by a flannel shirt tied in a knot. She also had a tie-dye bandana covering her jet-black hair with flaming red highlights.

"How's college treating you, Brandy?"

"Wonderful. I'm having a really good time."

"By good time, you mean partying, right?"

Brandy laughed and said, "Yes. There's that too."

"Does Sara know you're coming?"

"Nah, I want to surprise her."

"I see. So, do you always dress like a slut when walking down the road?"

Brandy got quiet. She sat there in disbelief.

Yerkes raised his voice. "Well, do you?!"

"EXCUSE ME! PULL THE CAR OVER – I WANT OUT!" Brandy shot back.

"Okay, no problem. Just asking a question," Yerkes replied. He pulled his cruiser over.

Brandy opened the door and got out. Suddenly, a chloroform rag was put over her mouth. She woke up to a pounding head and chained to the same ceiling beam Timber was first tied to in the old cabin.

Yerkes was sitting at a table drinking whiskey and admiring his new catch. Goblin walked into the room and said, "Very nice little addition to our game. Gordon will be pleased, I'm sure."

Brandy started screaming, "HELP! HELP! WHAT DO YOU WANT? LET ME GO! PLEASE LET ME GO!"

Goblin grabbed Brandy by the back of the neck and squeezed hard. "Relax, slut. No one can hear you out here, so it's a waste of time to scream. Plus, we will be starting the game soon and you can scream then." Yerkes and Goblin laughed together.

"Goblin, is the bitch still on the rack?" asked Yerkes.

"Yes. She's been very quiet. I think the broken ribs I gave her must really be hurting."

"Good. I have something to show her. Something that will make her very happy." Yerkes proceeded to show Goblin the pictures of Johnson's lifeless body.

Goblin laughed and said, "Yeah, right. Happy."

Yerkes went into the room holding Timber. "Hey, Deputy, you awake?"

What do you want, worm?" Timber responded.

"Oh, just to show you a few pictures."

"The only thing I want to see is the sheriff slap a pair of cuffs on your sorry ass."

Yerkes pushed on Timber's ribs. "Now, now, Timber. Play nice. After all, you're the new sheriff. For a little while, anyways."

"Bastard, keep your hands off of me. What are you talking about?"

Yerkes fumbled with a few cords and hooked the camera up to the monitor. "You ready to see your big, bad cowboy?" He turned the monitor on to show Timber Johnson's body just lying there.

Timber was horrified.

"Sorry to say, but I shot your sheriff three times in the chest and then watched him fall 20 feet to his death. It was such a beautiful thing to watch!"

Timber went crazy trying to break free. "I'M GOING TO KILL YOU. YOU HEAR ME, YOU FUCKING PIECE OF SHIT?"

Yerkes grabbed Timber by her face and said, "Look, bitch, the only thing you're going to do is regret becoming a deputy before you die. First day on the job and you're going to die. Must be a record of some kind."

Timber spit in his face. Yerkes raised his fist and was about to land a blow onto Timber's face when suddenly a commanding voice shouted out. "ENOUGH!" It was Commander Gordon. "We need her looking good for the game, you idiot. Millions of dollars are at stake. And you want to fuck that up? Don't ever let me see you do that again. You will have a chance when the game starts. Now, did you clean up your loose ends?"

Yerkes stumbled and spit out, "Yes, sir. Top County is secure. All we have to do is make the story fit the murders."

"Yerkes, I will figure that out and tell you how to proceed. It will be tricky, but first let's have some fun and make some money. I like your nice addition to the game. Will she be missed by anyone important?"

"No, sir. Just an out-of-town college tramp with a few friends in town that didn't know she was coming for a visit."

"Excellent, my boy. You just earned a $100,000 bonus. Now, let's get the electronic gear set up. Point the dish to these GPS settings." Gordon handed Yerkes a paper and then said, "Also, Ben, make sure the generator is gassed and behind the soundproof board. I don't want any clients hearing it. Ruins the mood."

Yerkes went on with his task.

Gordon turned his attention to Timber. He sighed and said, "What a shame. I really liked

Johnson. He saved my life three times. Did you know he was the top Federal Marshal in his field?"

Timber looked up and said, "Marshal?"

"Oh yes, my dear. One of the best. He cleaned up more corruption in small and big towns across this great land. But he wanted to settle down in his hometown and let his roots grow. Did you know he was the most loyal friend a person could have? Kind of sad, really. Especially to be terminated by the likes of Yerkes." He saw a tear roll down Timber's face. He gently put his finger on her cheek to catch it. "So sad. Deputy for one day and now you're going to die an unspeakable death. You should have been my little pet back at the academy, but it is what it is."

Timber stared at Johnson's picture. "I would rather have spent a few days with a real man like Sheriff Johnson than a lifetime with a little dick worm like you!"

"Fair enough, Timber. But that decision costed you your life. Now I must get ready for you to bring me millions of dollars today. I wish you a slow and agonizing death, my dear. And maybe after, I'll fuck the shit out of you just as you have your last heartbeat."

"You're a sick fuck!"

"Yes, I believe I am. Let me put the

pictures of your hero on auto-slide so you can enjoy watching them over and over." Gordon left the room. He approached Goblin and asked, "Did you get the place ready to go up in smoke?"

"Yes, Joe. The fire will be much hotter than the last one, for sure."

"Good. I don't want a fuck up! All evidence must be destroyed!"

"Sir, no worries."

"No worries? Two hikers almost brought down the whole operation. And you tell me not to worry!"

"Joe, that was a one-in-a-million chance of them coming along."

Gordon was slightly enraged. "One in a million?! That's what you said about Sheriff Taylor! You said – and I quote – 'Oh, boss, there is a one-in-a-million chance of Sheriff Taylor finding out anything.' And what happens? I get a fax from him. So, Goblin, do me a favor and NEVER say that to me again."

Goblin nodded and went about his tasks. Gordon went out for a walk and told Goblin and Yerkes that he was going to check the perimeter. But he just needed a private area out of ear shot to place a call.

"It's Gordon. Are you en route?"

"Yes, sir," replied the voice.

"Good. I don't want any witnesses. Kill them all."

"All, sir?"

"Yes. Yerkes, Goblin, and Torrington Dell, Jr."

The voice gasped and said, "Torrington, sir? Aren't we supposed to report to him when we get there?"

"Yes. Do everything as planned, but when he meets you at the meeting place, he will have Johnson's body with him. Yerkes somehow managed to kill him, so I want you to shoot Dell with Johnson's gun and make it look like Dell came to Top County for revenge and ran into Johnson, killing him. Leave the body there and in a day or two, I will personally come out to investigate. It will all go down as a deadly gun fight between the two. It's so fucked up, it's believable. And make the fuck sure you don't fuck this up! I have had enough fuck-ups to last a lifetime dealing with these clowns! Hurry up – I need you and your men here to secure the perimeter at the scheduled show time."

"Yes, sir. I'm on it. But question, sir. If Yerkes shot Johnson, Dell's gun won't match ballistics."

Gordon got furious. "I know that! Think I'm an idiot?! We will take care of that later today on our way out!" He ended the call.

Back at the cabin, Gordon discussed exactly where Johnson's body was with Yerkes. Yerkes was surprised by Gordon's interest, but Gordon calmed him. "Look, Yerkes. Johnson was shot three times – I think it's a good idea to bring the body here and burn it with the rest of the victims tonight," Gordon said.

"Sir, do you want me to go get Johnson?" asked Yerkes.

"No, my boy. I need you here. Plus, you earned a little play time with the girls. I'll have Dell pick the body and his truck up and bring them here."

Yerkes was happy with the plan. He told Gordon where to find Johnson's body and truck.

Gordon called Dell and told him the plan, except to bring both to the meeting spot where the rest of the crew will be. Dell agreed. Gordon lit up an expensive Cuban cigar and thought to himself, *How perfect this plan is. Perfect man, perfect plan.*

Goblin approached Gordon, who was napping on a hammock. "Sir, it's time. Everything is on and working. All the players are online."

Gordon placed a ski mask over his face so the bidders wouldn't recognize him.

"WELCOME TO THE TORTURE GAME! Tonight, we have a special surprise! We have two contestants – one a very young college student, and the main attraction: a beautiful female deputy sheriff!"

The screen went wild with players typing their approval. With their disdain toward law enforcement, it was a treat for them.

Gordon was excited because he knew the money was going to flow in. "Bidders, let's commence! Bidding on contestant number one!"

The camera turned on and Brandy saw herself in the monitor. She started to scream and shout, "PLEASE, PLEASE HELP ME!" She squirmed and wiggled against her bindings, but it was useless. She couldn't escape them.

Gordon said, "TIME! The winning bidder is number 72 for $100,000! Please type your request!"

A typed request came over the screen. *Insert a spider gag into her mouth and slowly stretch her mouth open until the jaw is maxed wide open.*

Brandy read the screen and fought her restraints once again. But it was no use. Timber could also read the monitor, but was helpless.

Goblin went behind Brandy and held her still while Yerkes placed the spider gag in her mouth. He turned the adjustment screw in slowly. Brandy was in pain from the corners of her mouth tearing. Yerkes stopped and stood back. The bidder typed his approval and Gordon thanked him for the wisdom to shut her up. Tears were flowing down Brandy's face. It was difficult for her to breathe and swallow.

Gordon went back to the screen. "Okay! Time for round two! Bidders, please place your bids!" The board went crazy. "The winning bidder is number 72! Again! At $90,000."

The typed request came in. *Rip her belly chain off.*

"Excellent request!" Gordon said. "Goblin, will you have the honors?"

Goblin grasped the chain firmly and ripped it right through her belly button skin. Blood shot out everywhere. For a brief moment, the bidders went wild. Brandy was twisting in pain, but was only hurting herself more.

Timber yelled from the back room, "YOU'RE A FUCKING BUNCH OF FREAKS WHO ARE NOTHING BUT A BUNCH OF PUSSIES! WHAT'S THE MATTER? VIAGRA DOESN'T WORK FOR YOU?"

The bidders heard Timber's outburst and became highly offended that a mere slut would address them in such a manner. Most were threatening to leave the game. Gordon asked what he could do to make it right and restore the honor. After a brief consultation, it was agreed that Timber will enter the game to be tortured simultaneously with Brandy.

Yerkes and Goblin went in to prep Timber for the game. They secured her to the rack, stood it upright, and wheeled her into the playing area next to Brandy. The bidders were ecstatic and liked what they saw.

Timber yelled, "YOU'RE ALL SICK FUCKS!"

A bidder chimed in, asking to speak. Gordon accepted number 20's request. "Hello, Deputy, can you hear me?"

Timber looked in the camera and said, "I hear you, you sick fuck!"

"Good. I will pay $5,000,000 to your host to have you flown to me and become my domestic slave. You will be treated fairly and live. Or you can die here tonight a very horrible and painful death."

"And what about Brandy?" Timber asked. "Will she be set free?"

The bidder laughed and said, "This offer is for your life – not hers. You have 20 seconds to accept or decline."

Gordon chimed in. "You would be a fool not to accept the offer," he told Timber.

Timber spit on Gordon's mask and yelled, "SO I CAN MAKE JOE GORDON OF THE MAINE STATE POLICE $5,000,000 RICHER? HERE'S MY OFFER: FUCK YOU!"

Gordon laughed and said, "I muted you with the controller in my hand. You do that again and I will end the game and put a bullet in your little friend's head. Understood, slut?"

Timber nodded because she knew he was serious.

Bidder 20 came back on and said, "I withdraw my offer."

Gordon thanked the bidder and continued the game. "Players, let the bidding start on the deputy. Who wants to be the first to torture her?"

The board lit up. Gordon let the bidding war go on for 10 seconds and then stopped it. "The high bidder is number 20 at $330,000!"

Bidder 20 typed his request. *Cut her clothes off in a humiliating way.*

Gordon looked at Yerkes and said, "You can take this one, boy. I have a feeling you will enjoy it."

"With pleasure, sir!" Yerkes picked up a pair of shears and whispered to Timber, "I wouldn't move an inch, bitch." He started by cutting her pant legs off and making her jeans into a thong. The bidders were enjoying her humiliation so much that some of them gave Yerkes a $5,000 bonus. Yerkes slowly slid his hand down what was left of Timber's jeans and yanked up her panties. They dug deep into her vagina. Her body jumped against the bindings. Yerkes cut them off and pulled them out fast. He stepped back so the viewers could enjoy the view. Timber's jeans were so short that most of her ass was exposed.

Bidder 10 chimed in and Gordon accepted the request. *I will add $100,000 to bidder 20's bid – if he accepts – to pin her badge to her bare breasts.*

Bidder 20 agreed and Yerkes ripped her shirt open and exposed a black-laced bra. "You slut!" he told her. Then he snipped her bra off. The bidding board lit up at the view of Timber's breasts. Yerkes asked Gordon if he'd rather the badge go through the nipple or the breasts.

Bidder 20 wrote, *Through the breast so the nipple can be exposed to further torture!*

Yerkes grinned as he pushed the pin through her breasts. Timber tensed up, but to her surprise, she didn't really feel much pain. But the humiliation was tormenting her and bringing back a flood of memories with Gordon. A tiny bit of blood trickled down her breasts and dripped off her nipple. The board lit up with the perverted bidders liking what they saw. Gordon told Yerkes to continue cutting her clothes off.

Yerkes was just about to completely remove Timber's cut-up shirt when a phone rang. The bidders heard the ringing and once again became nervous. The board lit up with the bidders questioning why a phone was ringing.

Gordon muted the mic and said, "Goblin! I gave an order of no phones on during the game!"

"Joe, it's not mine! See – mine is off," replied Goblin.

"Mine too, sir," Yerkes chimed in.

Gordon was not amused. "Then who's phone is it?!" The mysterious phone started ringing again. "It's coming from outside!"

"What the fuck!" responded Yerkes. "It's coming from my patrol car! And I know I turned everything off!"

Gordon was getting pissed. "Go see what it is, you idiot!"

Just as Yerkes touched the car door handle, the phone went off again. He jumped back in fear.

"WHAT ARE YOU, A PUSSY OR SOMETHING? GET THE FUCK OUT OF THE WAY!" Gordon yelled before opening up the car and finding the ringing cell phone in the back floor of Yerkes' patrol car. He held it up and said, "Whose fucking cell phone is this?!"

"Shit, sir, that must be Brandy's! It must've fell there when I grabbed her getting out of the car!"

The cell phone rang again. "Answer it as official business and tell whoever it is that you found the phone and you're looking for the owner," said Gordon.

Yerkes answered the phone and did as instructed. "Hello! Deputy Yerkes from the Top County Sheriff's Department." No one responded. Yerkes ended the call. "Sir, they must've thought they dialed the wrong number."

"Could be. Turn the phone off. We will deal with it later! We have a game to finish."

Half of the bidders left the game out of fear of getting caught, but the daring ones stayed. Gordon was hoping to save the game and make some money with what bidders were left.

"Okay, players! It's nothing of importance, but we forgot to turn off contestant one's cell phone. The game is secure and bidder 20 has left the game, so let's open a new bid!" He started the timer. "TIME! And the winning bidder is number five for a whopping

$500,000! Now we have some real game players!" Gordon appeared very pleased with the bid. "Bidder five, please type your request!"

The message came over the board. *Bull whip college girl's clothes off with razor barbs. All her clothes.*

The players lit the board up with approval. Brandy read the request and started to cry. Gordon handed Yerkes and Gordon both a bullwhip with six razor-filled tassels on the end. "Okay, men. One on each side of her – start whipping away!"

Timber screamed, "STOP! LEAVE HER ALONE! IT'S ME YOU HATE! YOU KNOW – THE COP! LET HER GO AND I WILL DO ANYTHING YOU WANT!"

Gordon laughed and said, "You are in no position to bargain, and you will do anything we say anyways." He made a fist and punched her in the gut. "There. That will shut her up while she fights for air. Now, gentlemen, please commence the whipping!"

Yerkes raised his arm and gave a wide forward stroke. The bullwhip made a loud snap as it landed on Brandy's breasts, ripping her shirt and bra and leaving claw marks. Goblin followed suit and ripped Brandy's bra, tearing into the tender skin of her breasts. Her body was trying to twist and turn, but the restraints were too tight and all she could do was suffer and wait for the next blow. Yerkes raised his arm and was about to unleash his next hit when suddenly the electronics went dead – monitor and camera. Even the lights. Everything was off and the satellite connection was gone.

"Fucking generator!" Goblin shouted. "I'll be right back!"

"Well this game is over!" Gordon told Yerkes. "At least I made a few bucks. Give me the cell phone we found."

Gordon walked over to Brandy. "Is this your cell phone, dear? Just nod for yes."

Brandy was almost in shock and didn't respond.

Gordon turned on the cell phone and looked at the call and text message list. Both were blank. He thought that was odd for a young girl, so he proceeded to check the contact list. While looking at it, he slowly sat in a chair almost in a daze.

Yerkes noticed Gordon's sullen look and asked, "What's wrong, sir?"

Gordon said nothing and just handed Yerkes the phone. Yerkes read the contact list. There were three numbers. His, Gordon's, and Goblin's. "What the fuck!" Yerkes exclaimed.

Gordon responded with one word: "Johnson."

17
AMBUSH

Gordon jumped to his feet. "Ben, did you check Johnson's body to see if it expired?"

"Sir, I did better than that! I took pictures. Didn't you see them on the monitor?" Yerkes answered.

"Yes, but I did not study them."

"I still have them on my phone. Here, look for yourself."

Gordon studied the pictures for a moment, and then said, "Ben, you have to be the worst law enforcement officer of all time! Here, look at your own fucking pictures and tell me what's missing."

Yerkes looked at the pictures and said, "I dunno – looks dead to me!"

Gordon smacked him in the head and asked, "You don't really know, do you?"

"Blood!" Timber mumbled. Gordon and Yerkes looked at Timber. "Blood. There's no blood. That's how I knew he was still alive. When dumb fuck showed me the pictures, I noticed it right away."

Yerkes turned to Gordon and said, "But, sir, his bulletproof vest was on his truck seat. I put bullets in his chest!"

Timber mustered up a laugh and said, "You fucking simpleton. He played you! That was my vest."

Gordon pulled his gun out and pointed it right at Yerkes' head. "I should kill you right now, you inept moron! But lucky for you I need to get out of here." Gordon called his cohorts that were on the move to kill Torrington Dell, Jr. No answer. Then he tried to call Dell.

Dell answered, "What?"

"Where are you, Dell?" Gordon asked. "I'm beating feet and getting out of here! And I suggest you do the same. Johnson's not dead!"

Dell didn't say anything and just ended the call.

Gordon got Quincy and told him to burn the Goblin mask with the rest of the place. "No evidence, no case. Let's make it big and hot and beat feet to my helicopter so we get the fuck out of here!"

"What about the girls, sir? Want me to kill them?" Quincy asked.

"No. Let them suffer and blow up with the cabin! Now move! I know Johnson – he's probably using his GPS on his phone to track this location. He can't be far behind."

Quincy went off to check the generator and came back to say, "Joe, it was all smashed to shit! Fuck!"

"That means Johnson's here already," Gordon said nervously. "Let's burn this place now! Let's roll!"

Yerkes and Quincy lit some large paper rolls on fire, which completely covered the cabin. Timber and Brandy frantically tried to get free, but couldn't.

Suddenly, something came flying through the window of the cabin. Yerkes picked it up and asked, "What the fuck is this?"

Gordon looked at him and answered, "It's the fucking tail rotor to my helicopter, you idiot!" Then he started to scream, "JOHNSON, SHOW YOURSELF! OR I'LL PUT A BULLET IN YOUR DEPUTY'S HEAD!"

BANG! BANG! Gordon, Yerkes, and Quincy dropped to the floor at the noise. Two canisters hit the floor and instantly filled the cabin with smoke. Gordon motioned Yerkes and Quincy into the other room and closed the room to get away from the tear gas and fire.

Quincy freaked out. "What are we going to do?! That Johnson is fucking nuts!"

Gordon looked at Quincy and said, "No, not nuts – smart. But I'm smarter. We are going to run out the front door guns blazing. Shoot anything that moves. And get to cover as quick as possible. He will never expect us to do that."

"But how do we know he's not in the front?" asked Yerkes.

"We don't know, you idiot! But Jesus Christ, he is only one guy. He can't save the girls and get us at the same time! And if I know him – which I do – he will try and save the girls. Okay, on the count of three: one, two-"

"WAIT! I don't have a gun!" Quincy interrupted.

Yerkes gave Quincy Timber's gun and said, "You do now."

Gordon yelled, "THREE!" and all three ran out shooting in every direction. They were met with no resistance. They decided to run to an old woodshed for cover.

Meanwhile, the old cabin was burning perfectly. Gordon turned to the other two men and said, "Watch the front – I'll go around back. Johnson will try to save the girls. The second you see him, unload on his ass. But this time shoot for his fucking head! He doesn't have much time before the cabin is fully engulfed, so be ready. Quincy, you go to the side by the vehicles and shoot anything that moves. And turn your phones on so we can communicate. Let's move!"

They all got into position to get the drop on Johnson. They waited and watched, but nothing happened. No movement, no nothing. The cabin was completely engulfed in fire and Gordon figured there was no way Johnson could possibly save the girls now. Gordon called Quincy and told him to meet him at the back of the shed.

When they met there, Yerkes was in a panic. "Where the fuck is he? What's he up to?"

Gordon yelled, "I have no idea, but let's get to the cars and get the hell out of here!"

They all hopped in Quincy's car, but the ignition was destroyed. "Fuck!" exclaimed Quincy.

Gordon told Yerkes to check his patrol car. The car started right up. "Johnson must have not had time to disable your car. Hit the gas, boy! And drive!"

Yerkes spun the tires and headed down the

narrow one mile dirt road just in time before the propane tanks blew the cabin to holy hell. Everything in and around it was completely destroyed. They turned their heads to look and broke out in laughter.

"Yee-haw! Evidence is gone for good!" Yerkes said. He turned his attention back to the road and hit the brakes in a panic.

There stood a woman with cut-off shorts, a man's unbuttoned flannel, and a cowboy hat covering her face. She was pointing a fully automatic M-16 machine gun straight at them. The three men were silent in disbelief as the woman pointed to each one of them, then used her finger to push up her hat.

Quincy was freaking out. "It's that crazy bitch!"

Gordon turned to Yerkes and said, "Earn your pay, boy! Get us the fuck out of here!"

Yerkes threw the car in reverse and stomped on the pedal. He backed up about 10 feet, then suddenly *CRASH!* He ran right into Sneaker's large push bumper on his tow truck.

Johnson walked out of the woods and joined Timber. He made an official statement. "Joe Gordon, Dr. Quincy Smith, and Ben Yerkes! You are all under arrest. Lay your weapons down, get out of the vehicle, and lay face down on the ground now!"

Yerkes yelled back, "OR WHAT?"

Johnson whispered to Timber, "You got this one?"

"Yes, I do, cowboy," Timber replied before yelling, "OR DIE!" at the three men in the car.

"Pat, it's Gordon. Let's talk. I can make you both very rich. And I mean retirement rich. Come on, Pat. You worked your ass off, and for what? To retire and die in some one-horse town? Come on, let's do this!"

"How much we talking?" Johnson asked.

Timber whispered, "What are you doing? You're not buying into this crap, are you?"

Johnson looked at Timber and said, "Don't you want to know how much he thinks his freedom is worth?"

"Well, cowboy, if I wasn't standing here half-naked with my ass cheeks playing peek-a-boo and three or four broken bones, then maybe I would like to know. But NO!"

Johnson gave his look and said, "Ass playing peek-a-boo?" He bended down behind Timber and looked. "Nice ass, Deputy. But I may have to cite you for a dress code violation."

Gordon got out of the patrol car and said, "Glad you came around. I can make you even richer if you join us."

"How much we talking to let you walk?"

"One million dollars. Untraceable notes in one hundred dollar bills. It's all yours, Pat."

"Where is the money, Joe?"

"It's hidden in my helicopter that you so graciously destroyed."

"NO DEAL, YOU MAGGOT!" screamed Timber.

"You answering for me now?" Johnson asked Timber.

"Shut up or I'll arrest you for obstruction!"

Johnson laughed. "I bet you would." Then he turned back to Gordon. "You heard the deputy, Gordon. No deal. Now on the ground!"

Gordon slowly moved his hand behind his back. Timber ripped a string of bullets about six inches from his feet.

"Okay, time's up, Gordon. Get on the fucking ground. Quincy and Yerkes, let's move it to the ground now or I'll have my bare-ass deputy open fire! I'm counting to five. ONE!"

Timber asked, "Bare-ass deputy?"

"TWO!"

Johnson whispered to Timber, "Tim, I just had to."

"THREE!"

"Do I really open fire?" asked Timber.

"FOUR!"

"Won't have to just pull the lever back now!"

"FIVE!"

"Okay, okay – don't shoot!"

All three men laid face down on the ground.

"Come on, boys! Spread eagle!" Timber demanded.

Johnson walked over and removed their weapons and pulled out a pair of handcuffs. "Joe, my friend, these are Timber's handcuffs. She asked me to put them on you." Johnson squeezed the cuffs around Gordon's wrists with extreme pressure.

Gordon yelled out in pain, lifted his head, and looked at Timber. "I'm going to kill you!"

Johnson kneed Gordon in the side and said, "There will be no more talk like that! Okay, Joe?"

Gordon went silent.

Johnson had all three men cuffed and on their feet. Sneaker threw a rope to Johnson and Johnson tied all three men together by their necks, leaving just enough room for them to walk. He turned to Gordon and said, "Joe, I have to ask: how many women have you killed with your sick, twisted game?"

"Pat, I have no idea what you are referring to. I'm sure you will give all the lack of evidence you have to my attorney," Gordon replied.

Brandy came walking out of the woods, went up to Yerkes, and kneed him in the nut sack. Yerkes doubled over in pain while Brandy headed over to Gordon. "Yes, he does, you piece of shit! See, I'm more special than one might think. I have a highly detailed photographic memory."

"So? Good for you," Gordon laughed.

"Yes, Joe. Good for Brandy," said Johnson. "And not so good for you. See, Brandy has a photo image of all of the bidders' IP addresses. That, Joe, was very stupid of you – to use them as identifiers. You may just be a walking, talking dead man when the bidders find out.

Gordon had fear in his eyes. "I'll turn everyone in and get into the witness protection program, smartass!"

Johnson gave Gordon his look and said, "No, you won't. We have everything we need to track them down without any help from you."

He turned to all three men. "Okay, fellas, let's take a short walk. My truck is just up the road." Johnson grabbed Gordon's arm and pushed him forward.

Johnson turned to Sneaker. "Bring up the rear!"

Sneaker fired up his old wrecker and yelled, "WITH PLEASURE!"

They were about to get into Johnson's truck when Gordon said, "Pat, I have six armed men in the area and they will be closing in soon. If you don't want your friends here to die, I suggest you let me go and bag these two idiots instead. Use them as scapegoats for old times' sake!" He stopped in his tracks and was in disbelief as he saw all six men kneeling in the road, head down and hands tied behind their backs.

"Joe, do you mean these guys?" Johnson asked.

Gordon looked and saw no one around except his men. He exploded. "WHAT THE FUCK?! YOU IDIOTS JUST STAY HERE TIED TOGETHER BY A LITTLE ROPE? WHAT THE FUCK WAS STOPPING YOU FROM LEAVING?"

Cough, cough, hack, spit. Bob Auld came out of the dark of the woods holding a rifle. He stopped to light a cigarette and said, "Me! That's who!"

Wally walked in front of Johnson's truck holding a pistol and said, "And me!"

Yerkes laughed at Gordon and said, "An old man and some burnt-out hippie are taking out your men!"

Wally walked up to Yerkes, jammed the barrel of his pistol into Yerkes' mouth and said, "NO ASSHOLE! It was just one man. Sheriff Patrick Johnson of the now uncorrupt Top County Sheriff's Department, who I am proud to be Honorary Deputy next to. One more word out of your ass-trap and I will shoot your voice box to fucktard land! Nod if you understand!"

Yerkes nodded.

"Wally, that's enough for now. Let's get Timber and Brandy to the hospital and the prisoners to the station," stated Johnson.

"Where are we putting these dirtbags? Holding cell only holds two, maybe three," Timber said.

A phone started ringing. It was coming from Gordon's front pocket. Timber walked over to Gordon and said, "Allow me" before sliding her hand into his front pocket and yanking down, putting Gordon in instant pain. "Oops, sorry about that. Grabbed the wrong thing!" She slid the phone out and handed it to Johnson. "I believe this is yours."

Johnson took the phone and said, "Hello, Betty!... You did?... Remind me to kiss you!" He then turned to the men. "Well, it looks like we have accommodations for you after all! Wally, tie them to the bumper of my truck. It's a long walk back for them. Brandy, you can ride in my truck. Sneaker, Wally, you bring up the rear. Mr. Auld, I believe you have a mission to accomplish."

"I do, my boy. See you all-" Bob said before he started coughing and hacking. He continued, "-later."

"Sheriff, would it be okay if I rode with Wally?" Brandy asked in a quiet voice.

Johnson looked at Wally and said, "Wow, Mr. Auld was right. Things do happen fast in Top County! Okay, let's roll!"

Johnson helped Timber into his truck and said, "Let's get you to the hospital."

"I'm all right, cowboy. It's just pain," Timber responded.

"Tim, you're one tough deputy."

"Well, I seen that nasty little fall you took. Are you okay?"

"I'm fine, but how did you see that?"

"Yerkes was so proud of himself that he took pictures and just had to show them to me. But I knew you weren't dead and that gave me the strength to stay alive."

"Are you going to continue to be my deputy? I will understand if you say no."

Timber was quiet for a second and looked at Johnson. "I was born for this job. Damn right I'll be your deputy after seeing and living through this! And I have to do my part to clean up all the scum out here. Washing dishes was not doing it!"

Johnson gave a small grin. "Do you like the hat I got you?"

"I actually do like the cowboy hat. I'll keep it forever!" As soon as Timber said that, she thought to herself, *And that's why he loves his hat — someone important gave it to him.*

Johnson looked at Timber as they had a connection of the minds and understood each other. He laughed and said, "Top County's new police dress code! Think the locals will warm up to seeing the Sheriff's Department in cowboy hats?"

"They will just have to now, won't they? Now, Mister, tell me how you didn't get hurt from taking that fall."

Johnson lifted his shirt.

"OMG! PAT!"

"Tim, it's just a little bruise."

"Bruise? Your whole side is bruised! You're seeing the doctor first!"

"Let's just see the doctor together."

Timber smiled and said, "Deal, cowboy."

In a low and serious voice, Johnson said, "Tim, did they. I mean, did you get…"

"No, Pat. Just mind-fucked. And, well, you can see the rest. But Gordon did rape me back at the academy and that's why I quit."

Johnson put his hand over Timber's chest and slammed on the brakes. He got out and saw a pile of men against his back bumper. He grabbed Gordon and said, "This is for Timber!" before punching Gordon in the gut. Johnson was known for his ability to throw a demanding fist.

Sneaker and Wally started laughing. Wally said, "Shit, he hit him harder than he hit me. And I'm still hurt!"

Johnson got back in his truck and hit the gas pedal. Gordon was being dragged until his cronies got him back on his feet. Timber curled up to Johnson's side and said, "My hero," and fell asleep. It was at least an hour back to town at walking speed.

18
SURPRISE

20 minutes into the trip, a large wood skidder used for pulling logs out of the woods pulled out in front of Johnson's truck and blocked the road. A man got out of the skidder and opened fire on Johnson's truck with a machine gun.

"TIM, GET DOWN!" Johnson yelled as he pushed her to the floor.

Sneaker hit reverse to give Johnson room to back up, but ended up crashing into another skidder behind him. They were trapped. Sneaker hit the floor board as bullets riddled past his head.

Wally grabbed Brandy and made a dash for the woods.

The guy toting the machine gun yelled out, "JOHNSON, ALL I WANT IS GORDON

AND HIS MEN. LET THEM GO AND I PROMISE TO KILL YOU AND YOUR FRIENDS QUICKLY WITH NO PAIN!"

Johnson told Timber to run for the woods once he started shooting.

"Pat, I'm not leaving you!"

"Deputy, that was an order. Now get ready."

Timber looked at Johnson and said softly, "Pat, I-"

Johnson cut her off. "I have a plan. Now get ready to run."

Timber gave him a quick kiss. "Yes, sir. I'm ready!"

"Okay, on the first shot, run deep into the woods." Johnson turned to the man. "NOT MUCH OF A DEAL! HOW ABOUT YOU AND YOUR MEN PUT YOUR WEAPONS DOWN OR I JUST KILL GORDON INSTEAD."

"SHERIFF, I DO TELL. YOU ARE AN OFFICER OF THE LAW AND I HAVE STUDIED YOU WELL. YOU WILL NOT KILL A HELPLESS PRISONER. NOW, YOU HAVE TWO MINUTES BEFORE I OPEN FIRE ON YOU AND YOUR FRIENDS."

"WHO AM I SPEAKING WITH?"

"JOHNSON, THAT IS OF LITTLE

CONSEQUENCE. BUT NO MATTER, YOU'RE ALREADY DEAD ANYWAYS. MY NAME IS TOM KICKER AND YOU'RE INTERFERING WITH MY LUCRATIVE BUSINESS. ONE MINUTE, SHERIFF."

Johnson turned to Timber. "Ready?"

"Yes."

"Okay, first shot." He yelled back to the man, "KICKER, HERE'S WHAT I'LL DO FOR YOU. WATCH YOUR HEAD COUNT ON THE MEN YOU THINK YOU'RE SAVING." Johnson quickly opened his door and fell to the ground where he had a perfect view of the prisoners' feet.

BANG! BANG! BANG! BANG! Johnson fired off four shots and four men fell to the ground yelling in pain. It took Kicker by surprise. Timber was able to make it into the woods. One of Kicker's men got one round off and shot Johnson in the arm before Sneaker shot and killed him.

"KICKER, YOUR BUDDY GORDON IS NEXT UNLESS YOU BACK THE FUCK OFF NOW!"

Kicker yelled, "WAIT!"

"NO WAITING, KICKER. BACK OFF NOW OR GORDON'S DEAD. AND FOR SOME REASON, I THINK YOU NEED

HIM ALIVE."

Kicker motioned for his men to back off and said, "OKAY, JOHNSON, I'M BACKING OFF! BUT YOU WILL NEVER MAKE IT TO TOWN ALIVE!"

Johnson yelled back, "SHAKE ME – I DON'T RATTLE!"

Kicker and his skidders disappeared into the woods. Gordon was freaking out at Johnson. "You can't just shoot people! You're as corrupt as I am!"

Sneaker came out of the woods clutching his rifle and said, "One dead."

Wally came out a few seconds later. He saw the sheriff's bloody arm and asked, "Are you okay?"

"Yes, thanks to Sneaker!" Johnson replied. "Wally, get these crybabies up 'n cram them into the back of my truck!"

Sneaker smashed out the bullet riddled windshield of Johnson's truck and said, "Kid, let's get out of here while we can."

Johnson nodded and instructed Wally, "Go get the girls and let's roll!"

Wally just stood there silent. Sneaker walked up to Wally and said, "Speak! Where are the girls?"

Wally was scared and nervous. "Brandy was freaking out, so Timber took her and said she knew a shortcut footpath to town. They're going to meet us there or get help."

Johnson and Sneaker looked at each other and then Wally. "Are you fucking stupid? Why would you let the girls go off on their own?!" Sneaker yelled.

Wally jumped back. "Look, Timber is a deputy sheriff and took charge! What was I supposed to do? She told me to come back here to help."

Johnson intervened. "Sneaker, I don't like it, but Wally is right. Now kiss and make up and let's get to town! I don't trust this Kicker asshole!"

Wally laughed and said, "You think?"

Johnson gave his look and said, "Get in and point your rifle at Gordon's head. If he moves, shoot him first."

Everyone hopped in and continued to town. They pulled up to the station and saw Betty and Willy, along with the rest of the town folk standing around a large round cage. Betty opened the cage door and motioned Johnson to back in. They unloaded the prisoners and drove out. Sneaker and Wally had their rifles drawn on the prisoners until Betty locked the cage door.

Wally ran over to Willy while Johnson turned to Betty. "Where did you get this cage?"

"It's the monkey cage from the old monkey house the town used to have!" Betty replied.

"Betty, I should kiss you."

"Pat, you're hurt! Are you okay?"

"Yes. Just a skim. Have you seen Timber and Brandy?"

"No. I thought they were with you!"

"They were, but a surprise player got the drop on us."

Gordon yelled, "HEY, MIGHTY SHERIFF, LOOK WHAT I GOT!"

Johnson looked over to see Gordon holding a small cardboard box. Sneaker pointed his rifle at Gordon. Johnson told the onlookers to go home.

Johnson was not amused. "Where did you get the box?"

Gordon laughed. "From a friend of ours." He opened the box and handed Johnson a note.

Sheriff,
I admire your tenacity and truly enjoy an intelligent adversary. But you will release Gordon in one hour or I will continue to play the game with your deputy and her little friend. Except this game will be cat and mouse. For every hour you do not release Gordon, I will send you a body part of your little bitches, starting with

fingers. Ever play chess, Sheriff? If you do, I believe I have you in check.
Your move.

Gordon held up Timber's badge and threw it to Johnson's feet. Sneaker and Wally looked at Johnson.

"What do we do now?" asked Wally.

Johnson picked up Timber's badge, cleaned it off, and put it in his pocket. "Find them," he said to everyone. "Sneaker, Wally, bring Yerkes to the holding cell in the station. I'll meet you there."

"Okay, Pat," said Sneaker. "Come on, Wally!"

The two men grabbed Yerkes roughly and pushed him down to the ground every few steps.

Johnson turned his attention to Gordon and said, "If they hurt one more hair on Tim, I will kill you!"

Gordon laughed. "And throw away your great career? I don't think so! You're not built that way."

Johnson pulled out his gun and shot Gordon in the foot. "I am now, Gordon. I found my home!" Johnson walked toward the station to the baseless screams and threats from a pissed off Gordon.

Johnson walked into the station and told Sneaker and Wally to tie Yerkes to the high ceiling beam. "Betty, I need you to get a doctor to look at Gordon's foot. It's bleeding. Make sure he sticks his foot out of the cage so no one goes inside."

"Okay, Sheriff," Betty responded.

"Oh, and Betty, shoot any of them that tries something stupid."

Betty grinned and said, "Yes, sir."

Johnson walked over to Yerkes, whose hands were tied over his head. He ripped his badge off his chest and said, "You're a total disgrace, kid. What are you – part of the 'me' generation?"

"FUCK YOU!" responded Yerkes. "What are you going to do? Beat me? Go ahead – there is a town full of witnesses that saw me come in here unharmed!"

"Yerkes, I'm not going to beat you. I just want information, like who gave Gordon that box!"

Yerkes laughed and said, "No way!"

"No way, huh?"

Sneaker broke a broom stick in half while Wally pulled Yerkes' pants down.

Yerkes was defiant. "You will never get away with beating me!"

Johnson looked at Yerkes in a comforting

way. "Ben, I'm not going to beat you. That would be too good for your sick ass – and leave marks! Instead, I'm going to impale you with the jagged edge of this broken broom stick." He looked Yerkes straight in the eyes, then turned to Wally and said, "Turn that video camera on and let's film this. Be interesting to let this slip on YouTube if we must." He looked back at Yerkes. "Now, Ben, I am only going to ask you this one more time. If you don't answer me, you're getting impaled. And I won't stop until you're just a whimpering shell of a man. Now, who slipped Gordon that box?"

Yerkes hesitated and Johnson walked behind him. Yerkes was unsure if Johnson was serious, but didn't want to take the chance. "TAYLOR!"

Johnson was stunned. "Come again?"

"SHERIFF TAYLOR'S WIFE!"

Johnson grabbed Yerkes by the neck. "Look, you fucking punk, I have had it with your bullshit."

"NO, NO, NO! IT'S TRUE! She set up Sheriff Taylor because she wanted him dead!"

"Why?"

"Why else, Sheriff? Money. He had a $1,000,000 life insurance policy. So she helped us and we helped her."

Johnson turned to his men. "Sneaker, Wally, go find Mrs. Taylor and bring her back here through the backdoor unnoticed. I don't want to tip off Kicker and crew. And hurry – we don't have much time!"

"Yes, sir," they said.

"Anything else you need to tell me?" Johnson asked Yerkes.

"Yes. The corruption in the marshal business runs very deep."

"Why do you say that?"

"Because even the great Sheriff Patrick Johnson is not by the book!"

"Maybe not, Ben, but I'm the better book to read. Come on in the cage!" Johnson threw Yerkes in the jail cell.

Yerkes yelled out, "HEY! WHAT ABOUT MY PANTS?!"

"Sorry, I have to keep them. I wouldn't want you to hang yourself. It's by the book!" Johnson poured coffee and went into his office.

Meanwhile, Timber was being held captive by Kicker and Dell. She was tied up to a skidder. While they were discussing a plan, Timber spent the time rubbing the rope that secured her to a sharp piece of steel. The rope broke and she was free. She quietly headed for the woods. She got about 50 yards before she heard Dell yell, "FUCK! THE BITCH GOT FREE!" She knew she couldn't outrun them with her broken ribs, so she hid under some loose brush and leaves. Dell walked right past her, but Kicker – being a born woodsman – spotted her quickly.

"Get out of there, bitch!" Kicker demanded.

Timber knew there was no sense in trying to fight or run, so she complied. Kicker grabbed her by the hair and walked her back to the skidder. "Dell, tie her to the front of my Hummer. Tie her feet to the winch plate and secure her hands to the hood tie downs."

Timber's back was arched over backwards on the hood in a painful position. Kicker pulled out his knife and cut the buttons to her flannel shirt, exposing her breasts.

"Get in, Dell! We are going to have a little fun!" Kicker started the Hummer and hit the gas. They went flying through the woods. Timber's body was getting whipped by tree branches and briar bushes. They crossed a mud pit and through a river and back to the skidder. Kicker cut Timber free and she fell to the ground. Her body was stinging from the ride.

"Dell, I think we took all the fight out of this bitch!" Both men laughed.

Dell went to his car and retrieved a pair of

suspension cuffs.

"What a great idea!" said Kicker. "Let's secure her to the skidder forks and suspend her off the ground." He ripped off the rest of Timber's shirt. "Hmm... nice, fine looking woman! Got a little meat on the bones – I like that!"

Dell was salivating at the mouth. "Let's fuck her and film it for Johnson!"

"All in due time, Dell. First we must free Gordon, kill Johnson, and clean up this mess. Then we will have some real fun with this bitch."

They both laughed as Kicker raised the skidder forks containing Timber. Her feet were about three feet off the ground and her hands were suspended.

Dell took a picture of her and said, "We will put this in the box for Mrs. Taylor to pick up. And when Johnson sees his deputy hanging like this, he will lose his fucking mind and stop thinking straight. Might just be the edge we need." He proceeded to take a few pictures of Timber's body – she was out cold from exhaustion.

"Sir?" said Dell.

"What is it?" asked Kicker.

"Why not make a video of her and send it on a memory card?"

"Great idea, my boy. How many memory cards do you have?"

"Plenty, sir. I take lots of videos!"

"Yes, I suppose being a perverted little fuck, you would. But I have a better idea. Roll the camcorder! I'm going to wake this bitch up. Make sure the volume is up!" Kicker picked up a switch from the ground and whipped it across Timber's back. She jumped to life and let out a scream. Kicker whipped Timber's back five more times and her stomach 10 times. Her skin welted up and her body fell limp again from the agonizing pain. Kicker looked directly into the camcorder and said, "Johnson, change of plans. If Gordon is not released in 10 minutes after you get this, I will whip your deputy 20 more times. And this will continue every delivery until she's dead. This just may be checkmate."

Kicker turned to Dell and said, "Bring the memory stick to the meeting point for Taylor.

Johnson was drinking coffee and trying to get back into the thinking mode when it hit him. He went back to Yerkes and said, "Ben, a lot of press will no doubt be here soon. Would you like your pants back?"

"Yes, I would," Yerkes answered.

"Then answer this: who came into Sheriff Taylor's office and sat in his chair the day you killed him?"

Yerkes got offended. "You mean my chair? I sat in my chair, in my office!"

Johnson walked back into his office and thought, *I needed to get this question answered in order to clear my mind.* But he already knew the answer. He also knew he needed a plan soon. Timber and Brandy's lives depended on it.

Suddenly, Betty came screaming through the door. "SHERIFF JOHNSON! SHERIFF JOHNSON!"

Johnson ran out of his office. "What's wrong, Betty?" He then saw Betty holding a terrified Brandy. She was wet, cold, and dirty. Johnson wrapped a blanket around her shaking body and brought her into his office. Betty went to make Brandy a cup of hot tea. Brandy clung onto Johnson and said nothing until Betty returned.

"Here you go, my dear," Betty said to Brandy. "Are you hungry?" Brandy nodded. "What would you like?"

"Cheeseburger, please," Brandy answered in a weak voice.

"Good idea, Betty. Have the diner bring over 20 cheeseburgers and fries as quick as they can. We could all use a bite to eat," Johnson instructed.

"Will do."

"Oh, and have the doctor tending to Gordon's foot come to my office. Quietly, please."

Brandy took a sip of the tea and started to cry. "She saved my life! You have to help her!"

"Brandy, relax. Breathe and tell me what happened," soothed Johnson.

"We were trying to get back to town when we heard a couple of four wheelers. We were running toward them for help, but realized they were the same men that stopped us on the road. They saw us, but Timber hid me and told me what direction led to town. After she drew them away, she ran off in another direction. I heard screaming and knew they got her. I should have stayed with her! She's probably dead by now and it's all my fault!"

"Brandy, Tim's not dead. They need her alive to trade for Gordon. For some reason, I haven't figured out why they really want him. I'm sure it has nothing to do with being a comrade."

"I know why. When they had me chained to the ceiling, I saw a bunch of numbers on another monitor. And whenever a player won a bid, the dollar sign would go up next to the numbers. I'm pretty sure they were the bank account numbers for banks in Switzerland because Goblin said something about going to

Switzerland."

"Brandy, I think you found the missing piece of the puzzle! I sure would like to get my hands on them numbers. It would be the perfect bargaining tool needed to help Tim."

"I have the numbers in my mind. Photographic memory, remember?"

"I remember. I just don't want to pressure you. You have been through a lot."

"Give me some paper and I'll write them down for you."

"Brandy, you're awesome. I hope you know that. You may have just saved Timber's life. See, it was the right thing to do coming into town."

Brandy forced a smile and wrote the numbers down. Betty came in with a bag full of cheeseburgers and fries at the same time Sneaker and Wally brought Mrs. Taylor in.

Johnson met them and said, "Wally, Brandy is in my office if you want to see her." Wally made a dash for the office, but not in time for Johnson to grab him by the arm. "Ask her no questions about her ordeal, okay?"

"Yes, Sheriff. I understand," replied Wally.

Johnson walked in to see Wally giving Brandy a big hug. He grabbed the numbers that Brandy wrote down and winked at her. He closed the office door so her and Wally could be alone.

"What is the meaning of dragging me here by these ruffings? You should be ashamed of yourself! If Andy was alive, he-" started Mrs. Taylor.

Johnson interrupted, "Would do the same thing? Now calm down, Mrs. Taylor, and skip the theatrics. We know you're involved in your husband's death. So tell me, was it just for the love of money?"

Taylor's voice hardened. "That's right! It was for the money! I never wanted to move up here in this frozen tundra with five feet of snow every winter! And I was sick of his police work – that's all he ever cared about. So yeah, it was time for me to live!"

"Yeah, in prison!" Sneaker said as he cuffed her to the desk.

"Wait! Sheriff, I want to make a deal!" pleaded Taylor.

Johnson grinned because he knew she would cave at the thought of prison. "What do you have to offer, Mrs. Taylor?"

"I'm supposed to pick up a box and bring it to Gordon. If I tell you where the pick-up location is, will you let me go?"

Johnson gave his look and said, "Not a chance! But the information may get you out of the death penalty for the murder of a Federal

Marshal!"

"Really, Patrick? I'm 15 years younger than Andy! I'll testify to years of mental and physical anguish, and to having temporary insanity for being stuck out here! Just lost my mind and snapped! I'll be out in no time!"

"Don't hold your breath! But it may help if I report that you came to your senses and were very cooperative in helping the investigation."

"Fine. It's at the old cider mill. There's an outhouse – it will be in there."

"How does Kicker contact you?"

"It's a prearranged pick-up spot. He only calls if there is a change in plans. And you better hurry – the pick-up is on the hour, every hour. And if I don't do the pick-up, your little girlie friend will no doubt be in big trouble."

Johnson turned to Sneaker and said, "Stay here. Eat some food and keep an eye on things. I'll be right back." He grabbed a few cheeseburgers and headed for the door. Then stopped. "Mrs. Taylor, do you have Kicker's phone number?"

"No, he only calls with a restricted number," Taylor answered.

"To your phone number?" Sneaker asked.

Taylor nodded. Sneaker went through her purse and threw Johnson her cell phone. "Hey! You can't take my phone!"

"I'm not – I'm just borrowing it!" Johnson said before heading out.

Yerkes shouted down, "HEY! SNEAKER, GIVE ME ONE OF THEM CHEESEBURGERS!"

Sneaker looked at Yerkes and said, "Not until Timber is safe, you prick!"

"Oh, Sneaker. I love it when you're so forceful," Betty said with a twinkle in her eye.

Sneaker turned tomato red and said, "Why you sexy, cute police dispatcher! You done embarrassed me!"

Betty smiled and said, "Just eat your lunch!"

Meanwhile, Kicker needed to check on a few things. He told Dell, "I'll be back in about 20 minutes. Keep an eye on the bitch!"

Once Kicker was gone, Dell eyed Timber. Her body hanging there topless with her breasts exposed and in ripped cut-off jeans was more than the pervert could handle. He walked up to the skidder, lowered the forks just enough for Timber's toes to touch the ground, and started fondling her breasts. He pinched her nipples so hard that it made her jerk to life. "Oh, the little slut is awake now!" He continued to pinch and twist her nipples. "I'm going to have fun with you after we kill your sheriff boyfriend! I think I'm going to keep you for myself in a private dungeon in New York. I'll torture you on a daily basis until you completely submit to me as a slave!"

Timber spoke up in a weak yet defiant voice. "Sounds like fun, little man!"

Dell became enraged and grabbed Timber by the nipples and pulled her forward as far as the rope securing her would let him. He let go and Timber's body slammed backward into the hard steel of the skidder, knocking her out.

Suddenly, Dell heard a voice. "HEY! WHAT'S GOING ON HERE?" Dell turned to see a large man standing in front of him. It was Johnson's friend, Simon – the fire marshal. He looked at Timber's half-naked body.

"Hot, isn't she?" Dell said.

Simon exploded with anger. "YOU FUCKING DIRTBAG." He grabbed Dell and swung him around right into the skidder, face first into the hard steel. He picked Dell up over his head and slammed him onto the ground. Dell was no match for Simon's strength.

Dell reached for his pistol, but Simon grabbed his arm and slowly lifted Dell off the ground. Simon took the pistol from him with his other arm and hit Dell across the face with it, busting his nose into pieces. Dell's body went limp like a rag dog and fell to the ground.

"TIMBER! TIMBER! I'LL GET YOU

DOWN!" Simon yelled.

He reached in his pocket and pulled out a pocket knife. He was just about to cut Timber's body down when he heard, "FREEZE!"

Simon turned around to see Kicker. "I should have known."

Kicker just laughed. "I love the stupid hicks in the sticks – so damn predictable. Nice job on Dell. Saved me the trouble of killing him later. You did kill him, right?"

"I hope so," Simon quipped.

"Okay, move away from the little bitch or I'll shoot you where you stand."

Simon walked one way and Kicker the other. They made a circle. Kicker ended up next to Timber. He gave her a push. "She's still out cold! Cute little thing – wouldn't you agree, big man?"

"Look, dirtbag. I have no idea what's going on, but I advise you to cut her down!"

"Or what?"

Timber yelled, "OR THIS!" as she gathered up all her strength, raised her feet, and pushed Kicker in the center of his back as hard as she could, sending him into the skidder.

Simon launched toward Kicker, knocked the gun out of his hand, and tried to tackle him to the ground. Kicker managed to twist free and get to his feet. He kicked Simon in the face.

He tried to kick him again, but this time Simon grabbed his foot and twisted it hard enough for Kicker to fall to the ground. Simon wasted no time and plummeted him.

Simon threw a right and left that landed on Kicker's jaw, then unloaded a barrage of massive right and left hand blows to Kicker's face. He kept hitting Kicker's face over and over again until it was a bloody pulp and his body was lifeless.

Simon stumbled to his feet and walked over to Timber. She let out a laugh and said, "I guess you really do know how to put out a fire."

Simon began to cut her down when suddenly *BANG! BANG!* He turned around to see Dell standing in front of him holding a gun. Simon fell to one knee before Dell said, "Bye, bye!" and shot him in the chest one last time. Simon's massive body fell limp.

"YOU FUCKER!" Timber screamed.

Dell grabbed her by the head and bounced it off the skidder, putting Timber back in la-la-land.

Kicker started to regain consciousness and wiped the blood from his eyes. He looked around and saw the carnage. "Good job, kid! That fucking monster was one tough hick!"

Dell laughed. "You think? But not tough

enough for three bullets. Two in the back, one in the front!"

"Dell, it's time we quicken the pace!"

19
SHOWDOWN

Johnson arrived at the old cider mill and found the outhouse. He took the memory stick to his truck and played it on his computer. He watched as Timber was put through hell. He became enraged. But he knew to stay focused. This was new ground for him because he never cared for people in other cases the way he did at that moment. Mrs. Taylor's phone started to ring. Johnson looked at it to see a restricted number. *Okay, it's time for the showdown!*

"Kicker, it's Johnson," Johnson answered.

Kicker was stunned. "Well, if it's not the mighty Sheriff Johnson! Since you have Taylor's phone, I'm sure you know all about her involvement and no doubt have seen the memory stick."

"I do. And I did."

"Good. Then you know what's going to happen next if I don't see Gordon very soon. Oh, and by the way, your friend – the fire marshal – tried to play hero. He did a pretty good job, too. But all he got for it was dead! But I still have two bargaining chips."

"No, Kicker, you have one. Brandy is safe and sound at the station."

"No matter. I don't need her!"

Johnson gave a hearty laugh and said, "Yes, you do, you dumb fuck! She has a photographic memory and I have all the bank account numbers you need to retrieve your money from Switzerland. I also know the exact amounts! Gordon was stupid enough to display them on another screen so he could make sure the bidders' money was, in fact, being transferred!"

Kicker yelled, "GORDON'S A FUCKING IDIOT! Okay, Johnson – a trade then. Your deputy for my bank account numbers. And once the money is confirmed, you may have your precious Timber."

"Okay, Kicker. You, me, and Tim. No one else."

"No problem, Johnson. Your fire marshal took care of Dell, so it's down to just me and you. Meet me at Gordon's helicopter in 20 minutes. And Johnson, one trick – just one –

and she dies! Understood?"

"Yes," Johnson said before ending the call. He headed to his truck and started toward the meeting point.

Kicker cut Timber down and tied her hands to the back of his four wheeler. "Hope you can keep up!" He proceeded to drag her through the muddy woods, causing her intense pain.

Johnson got there first. He heard the four wheeler approaching. Kicker came into the clearing, showcasing Timber's muddy, bloody body being dragged for Johnson.

Kicker turned off the vehicle and said, "Is this the bitch you're looking for?"

Johnson had enough. He made his move toward Kicker, but stopped as a voice came from the helicopter.

"FREEZE, LAW MAN!" Dell screamed.

Kicker broke out in laughter. "See what happens when you think with your heart, Johnson? You all get killed! And I do believe I have you in checkmate!"

"Is she alive?" Johnson asked.

"I don't know! Go look."

Johnson ran over to Timber. She whispered, "I'm alive, cowboy" to him as he cut her free and put his jacket over her.

"Okay, Johnson, enough! Throw your

weapon to Dell!" Kicker demanded.

Johnson did as instructed.

"And your ankle gun!"

Johnson reached down and threw his other gun.

"Good boy. Now, be a dear and give me the bank account numbers!"

Johnson pulled out a piece of paper and handed it to Kicker.

"Johnson! I said no tricks! Where are the other numbers?"

"You verify that one and I'll tell you the other ones after my deputy is set free!"

"No deal, Johnson."

"Fine. Then kill us both and you lose tens of millions of dollars!"

Kicker entered the numbers into his pocket computer, hit a few buttons, and transferred the money into his account. He smiled at Dell. "$3,000,000 just transferred to my offshore account! You know, Johnson, maybe I will just run with the money and kill you both."

"You won't, Kicker. You're too greedy!"

Dell chimed in, "Sir, why not just let her go? How far can she get in her condition? We have more than enough time to fly out of here."

"Fine. The bitch can go."

Johnson walked over to Timber and helped her to her feet, gave her a hug, and whispered, "Be safe, Tim."

"You, too, cowboy," Timber said as she slowly disappeared into the woods.

Johnson gave Kicker the rest of the bank account numbers. Kicker was all smiles as he punched the numbers into his computer and transferred all of the money.

"Ah, $32,000,000. All safe and secure in my accounts. Johnson, it's been fun. Dell, kill him!"

"Not so fast," Johnson said. "See, I found your getaway flying machine and disabled it as insurance. And we both know you will never be able to drive out of Top County alive. So, Kicker, your almost-checkmate just turned into a check! Your move."

"Sir, I'll beat it out of him!" offered Dell.

"No, you won't, Dell," responded Kicker. "Guys like Johnson don't give in that way. I'll take him to my helicopter and you jump on my four wheeler and hunt that bitch down. Drag her back to meet us."

Dell was all smiles as he hopped on the vehicle and drove after Timber.

Kicker turned to Johnson and said, "Come on, Sheriff. I do believe you know the way. I must say your deputy is one tough broad. I'm going to enjoy killing her."

Johnson gave his look and kept walking.

They arrived at Kicker's helicopter and Kicker examined the missing fuses. "Very well played, Johnson!"

"You're going to kill Dell before you leave here, right?" asked Johnson.

"No, I'm going to kill you all before I leave here. Just like your meddling fire marshal!

"By the look of yours and Dell's faces, I'm going to have to say he had a little fun first!"

Kicker pointed his gun at Johnson and said, "Don't provoke me, Sheriff! As you know, I'm a bit unstable."

"No, Kicker, you are a lot unstable!"

Suddenly, they heard a four wheeler coming at high speed through the woods. Kicker laughed. "You may not want your deputy now. Seems like Dell is tearing her up pretty good!" It came into the clearing dragging a body and crashed into the side of Kicker's chopper. They recognized it as Dell's dead body.

Johnson charged at Kicker. Kicker spun around and managed to squeeze out a round. He hit Johnson in his right arm just as Johnson tackled him to the ground. The two men wrestled around. Kicker got to his feet first and searched for his gun, but couldn't find it in time before Johnson got to his feet.

"Okay, Johnson, let's do this! Man-to-man! How's the right arm? I do believe this fight is in my favor," Kicker said.

Kicker landed a right jab to Johnson's gut, then grabbed his wounded right arm and twisted it. He swung Johnson around and slammed his body into a large maple tree. Johnson was able to turn his head away from the tree in time, but took a massive body slam. Kicker unleashed a series of right and left hits into Johnson's gut. Then a hard right hit to his face. Johnson was leaning against the tree when Kicker grabbed Johnson by the chin with his left hand and said, "Goodbye, Sheriff" before throwing a very hard right hit toward Johnson's face. Johnson made Kicker believe he was getting weak, but he moved out of the way quick enough to have Kicker's fist plummet into the hard tree. The impact broke several of Kicker's fingers and his wrist. He bent over in pain, holding his right hand.

Johnson regained his stance and told Kicker, "Looks like a fair fight now!" He hit kicker in the side of the face with his dominant arm. Kicker returned to his feet because Johnson let him. Johnson began circling him like prey. Kicker swung a lame left hit, which Johnson side-stepped. Johnson punched

Kicker in the face a couple of times until it was a bloody mess. Johnson wound-up his left arm and hit the side of Kicker's jaw, making blood splatter everywhere, along with a few teeth. Kicker's jaw broke in half with a large *CRACK!* before his body hit the ground.

Johnson ran over to Dell to see if he was alive. He wasn't. Johnson yelled out for Timber. *BAM!* Johnson heard a gunshot. He turned to see Kicker pointing a gun at him.

Timber came limping out of the woods from behind Kicker, walked in front of him, and said a single word: "Checkmate." Kicker fell to the ground with one gunshot wound to the back of the head.

Johnson ran over to Timber. They embraced each other for a few minutes. "Cowboy, next time you slip me a gun, make sure it has more than one bullet in it!"

"Why, Deputy? You only needed one!"

Timber looked at Johnson and said, "I would punch you, but I'm too weak."

Johnson gave her his look and said, "Let's get out of here!"

Johnson and Timber rolled into town and immediately saw the media and their cameras set up everywhere. Before they could drive by, they were swarmed by reporters.

"SHERIFF! SHERIFF! ANYTHING TO

SAY?!" one reporter asked.

"Yes. Go talk to my dispatcher, Betty. She handles the press and has the full story," replied Johnson.

As the reporters rushed over to the front of the station, Sneaker, Wally, Willy, and Brandy went running out the back. Johnson and Timber looked at each other and tried not to laugh because of how much they were hurting.

"Come on, let's get you to the hospital!" Johnson said to Timber.

"Good idea, cowboy."

"Tim, I'm still writing you up for a dress code violation!"

"Hey! What for? I have a Top County-issued police jacket on!" They tried to laugh again, but couldn't.

At the hospital, an orderly brought Timber into one room and Johnson into the other. Before Timber entered her room, she heard Johnson say, "Hey, Tim!" before throwing something her way. She caught it with one hand. "Make sure they bill the county!" She looked at what she had caught and saw it was her badge.

"Damn right!" Timber replied before going into her room.

Johnson made a call while waiting for the

doctor. He called Mike Baker and asked, "You en route?"

"Yep! Should be at your office in two hours," Mike replied.

"Okay, great. See you there. Oh, and Mike? You may want to use the backdoor."

"Gotcha. Thanks."

Johnson got a call from Sneaker. "Gordon escaped!"

Johnson didn't seem surprised. "How?"

"Cohort pretended to be the media, and in all of the confusion, he got Gordon out and gave him a gun. We have him in custody, but Gordon got away. What do you want us to do?"

"Clear the media out from the cage. Tape it off in a 100 foot perimeter and shoot anyone who crosses it. You and Wally guard it until the marshals show up. I'll get Gordon!"

"Pat, be careful!"

Johnson let the doctor bandage him up and left against his orders. Johnson figured Gordon was on his way to Kicker's chopper, so he pulled up to the clearing. He saw Gordon, who told Johnson to put his gun down.

"Why?" questioned Johnson.

An injured, but very much alive fire marshal came out from behind the chopper with Gordon's gun pointed at his head.

"Simon, you're alive?!" exclaimed Johnson. Simon, in pain, gave a weak nod.

"Sheriff, I found him walking to town as I was driving out. Now put your gun down or he dies. And give me the missing fuses. This time you have 10 seconds to comply!"

"Gordon, you might want to look behind you."

"Nice try, Johnson. Five seconds."

Simon was 10 feet from Gordon and knew he couldn't reach him without getting shot again, but he thought quick and reached up for the rotor of the small chopper and spun it at Gordon.

Gordon ducked down and *BANG!* Johnson shot him in the chest. Gordon fell to the ground, crawled to the maple tree, and sat against it. He looked at the carnage and all of his dead friends.

Johnson walked up to him. Gordon raised his gun to shoot Johnson. "Put your gun down! It's over!" Johnson said.

"Pat, I'm not going to jail," said Gordon before turning the gun on himself and squeezing the trigger. Blood and brains splattered everywhere.

Johnson said just two words: "CASE CLOSED!"

Johnson turned to Simon and suggested

taking him to the hospital.

"Good idea, Pat. I feel like shit and you look like shit!" Both men laughed. "Tell you what – you can have this police business. I'll stick to fires."

"Simon, I want to thank you for everything you did to help Tim."

"Anytime, Pat."

They arrived at the hospital and Johnson checked Simon in. He wanted to check Timber's room, but decided she must be sleeping and headed to the office to meet Mike, instead.

Mike was waiting for Johnson when he arrived. "Jesus, Pat! You look like you were in a battlefield! You alright?" asked Mike.

"I'm fine, Mike. It's been a long couple of days on the job," Johnson explained.

"What the hell happened here, anyways?"

"Sit down, Mike, and I'll tell you the whole story."

After several hours of chatting, Johnson unfolded the whole story. Mike was just silent. Johnson handed over all of the evidence and IP addresses and thanked Mike for taking over from there.

"You want in on the hunt to find the bidders?" asked Mike.

"No. I have work to do in Top County. I'm

staying home for good," replied Johnson.

"Okay, Pat. We will miss you, for sure. But I will make sure we get those bastards for you and your town."

"Yes. My town. I like the ring of that," Johnson said smiling. They shook hands. "Mike, get these scumbags out of my county! I'm going home."

"I'm on it."

"Thanks, and lock up when you're done." Johnson stopped and told Mrs. Taylor and Yerkes, "I hope it was all worth it for you two."

"Sheriff, you find anything of value in my house?" Yerkes asked.

"Nope, it was ransacked when I got there. I suspect Kicker beat me to it!" answered Johnson.

On his way past the monkey cage, he saw the town got wind of what had happened. The prisoners were covered in paint and egg. They clapped as Johnson walked by. "SHERIFF! SHERIFF! SHERIFF!" they began to chant.

Mr. Hammond gave Johnson a bag and said, "Enjoy the chicken!"

Johnson nodded, got in his bullet-riddled truck, and headed home. He looked behind at all of the federal marshals standing around. He laughed and turned on the main road. He passed the meat wagon sent to pick up Kicker and Gordon's bodies. He was tired, hungry, and pretty beat up, but thought about everything Timber went through.

He pulled into his driveway and was amazed that all of the tree branches were cut. His house came into view and so did Bob, Betty, Sneaker, Wally, Willy, and Brandy. He got out of his truck to a hero's welcome, but stopped them short. "I'm no hero! You guys are! I couldn't have done it without you."

Timber came limping out of the front door. "Hey, cowboy!"

"Tim!" Johnson exclaimed. He ran to hug her. "Why are you not in the hospital?"

"I'm not the hospital type! Besides, all I need is fresh air and rest."

Sneaker cleared his throat and said, "Your deputy heard about Gordon's escape. We caught her trying to go help you, so we brought her here."

Johnson gave her his look and shook his head. They fired up the grill and partied. Johnson finally felt like he was home.

20
NEW BEGINNINGS

The next three weeks, the Smally brothers helped Mr. Auld fix up Johnson's barn, clear his pasture, and paint his house.

One day, Sheriff Johnson and Deputy Tim made a special call to Wally and Willy. They arrived at the Smally house greeted by the brothers and Brandy, who were glad to see them.

Johnson and Timber got out of the vehicle with straight faces and said, "This is official business! I'm afraid your life of leisure is over. We have a letter here from the Governor of Maine pardoning you both of all crimes you were falsely accused of."

"What does that mean?" asked Wally.

"It means you have no criminal record – all traces of it have been erased. In other words: it never happened!" exclaimed Timber.

Wally, Willy, and Brandy jumped for joy and hugged each other.

"Boys, you are free to make your dream of helping children with special needs a reality! And I hope you do it right here in Top County!" said Johnson.

"Sheriff, with all due respect, we no longer have our land or money to pursue our dream," Wally said with tears in his eyes.

Johnson motioned to someone in his truck. A well-dressed woman got out and walked over. "Fellas, this is Carol Cress from the Bureau of Federal Land Management. Wally and Willy Smally, on behalf of our agency, we have investigated the way Tom Kicker embezzled land from the people of Top County. I present you with a deed for all the land that you lost. Your ownership is now restored. All you have to do is file this paperwork with us before next Wednesday. Think you can do that?"

Timber motioned Brandy to go into the house and let the boys talk. They looked over the paper. When they came back out, Brandy whispered something to Wally and Willy, making their eyes light up.

"Yes! We will do it!" they exclaimed. They shook Johnson and Carol's hands frantically with tears in their eyes.

"Here's my number. If you need anything at all, just call me," said Carol. "I have a child with special needs and I will ensure he's your first camper. Now get to work, boys!"

Johnson, Timber, and Carol hopped in Johnson's truck and left.

That night, Johnson and Timber were sitting on a newly installed two-seater porch swing under the warm star-lit night. They were enjoying Johnson's favorite beer: Narragansett. Timber looked at Johnson's rugged facial features through the light of the moon and couldn't help but notice how relaxed he was.

"Cowboy," she whispered, "you know you're just a big soft-y, right? Giving Wally and Willy that $500,000 you confiscated and clearing their names. You did God's work!"

Johnson kissed Timber on the head and said, "No, Tim, not God's work. It was simply the right thing to do. Injustice to justice. The final move in the chess game.

Timber looked confused. "The final move?" she asked.

Johnson got up and headed for the kitchen door. "You know, pick up the pieces and put away the game."

Timber chased him into the house. A few minutes later, the only light from inside the house went off.

RING, RING, RING! the phone rang. Johnson got up to answer it. "Hello?"

"Sheriff, it's Betty. There is a disturbance down at the Broken Branch Saloon!"

"Of course there is," Timber grumbled.

ABOUT THE AUTHOR

K. N. Messier is an avid explorer of old-time places, such as ghost towns and abandoned structures deep off the well-used path. Though their stories have long been forgotten, their remains inspire K. N. Messier to bring forth a story of fiction and put into words what make them unique. The product is an exciting novel filled with mystery and unimaginable excitement in every horrific turn of the page.

K. N. Messier has experience in ghostwriting, as well as playing a character in an indie film – both of which fueled his passion to create the miniseries of novels known as TOP COUNTY. Living in the great state of Maine has offered K. N. Messier an abundance of imagination. Follow him as he takes you through his twisted and demented mind and unravels all of his thoughts into an unforgettable adventure!

You can contact K. N. Messier at
TopCounty@yahoo.com

Made in the USA
Lexington, KY
03 May 2018